Sofra Cookbook

Sofra Cookbook

Modern Turkish and Middle-Eastern Cookery

Hüseyin Özer

Thorsons
An Imprint of HarperCollins*Publishers*

Thorsons
An Imprint of HarperCollins*Publishers*
77–85 Fulham Palace Road
Hammersmith, London W6 8JB

Published by Thorsons 1998

1 3 5 7 9 10 8 6 4 2

© Hüseyin Özer 1998

Hüseyin Özer asserts the moral right to
be identified as the author of this work

Copy Editor: Alexandra Carlier

Photographer: John Turner

A catalogue record for this book is available
from the British Library

ISBN 0 7225 3682 8

Printed and bound in Great Britain by
Woolnough Bookbinding Limited, Irthlingborough, Northants

Contents

Acknowledgements

In the first instance, I would like to thank Wanda Whiteley, Senior Editor at Thorsons, for persuading me to write this book. Next, my sincere thanks must surely go to my kitchen brigade and staff.

Introduction

Early morning visitors to the Sofra restaurant kitchens often remark upon the cheerful sound of the chefs' singing. They are usually singing an eclectic mix of Turkish, Middle Eastern and Asiatic songs; and it provides a melodious foreground to the background rhythms of knife blades rocking on chopping blocks. As the chefs sing and chop the overflowing daily deliveries of fresh herbs and vegetables, so green mountains of feathery dill and flat-leaf parsley gradually emerge on the counters and grow ever higher against the tall stainless steel backdrop. Sometimes, these emerald mountains are offset by a red carpet of chopped tomatoes and peppers. I often muse that this daily scene encapsulates all the key elements of Sofra's cuisine: it is carefree, simple, honest and vibrant. It begs no special skills beyond a respect for ultra-fresh, healthy ingredients. And it is as eclectic as the songs being sung.

Although Sofra food may refer back to a Turkish heritage, it also looks forward, unashamedly, to international developments in food styles – especially those influenced by the Orient – and to trends in healthier eating. Anyone who expects Sofra to deliver what they consider to be 'typically Turkish' food, with echoes of a doner-kebab bar, will be sorely disappointed. When I look to Turkey for inspiration, my glance is directed more towards regional home-cooking traditions than to restaurant fare. Even so, I do not cling to a Turkish heritage as though it were static. Rather, I try to respond to the mood of the times, just as the innovative cooks of the Ottoman empire did when they adopted and adapted the foreign cuisines of the imperial conquests. Turkish history reminds me that, for generations, Istanbul was the centre of trade, especially in spice, between east and west, north and south, so its markets were a forum for the cross-cultural exchange of culinary ideas.

The contemporary trend towards a healthier diet has changed most people's eating habits, including my own. That said, some well-balanced diets are frankly dull; and I am not content unless my diet has been elevated, beyond that somewhat bland classification of 'light and healthy', to the realms of bright allure. Yes, I want to feel alert and energized, fit and healthy, but I also covet sensuous food with exciting, racy tastes and interesting textures. Vegetables and salads must be so fresh as to be ravishing. Starters and meze must burst with lively flavours or with an exuberance of fresh herbs. Pasta must by luscious and moist. Fish, chicken and lamb must be subtly, but tantalizingly, spiced. I'm not sure whether there exists a category of food which might validly be termed aphrodisiac (the sultans of ancient history would, of course, have said that there does) but I am convinced that naturally beautiful food, with its abundant vitamins intact, arouses that vital feel-good factor.

Fresh, natural flavours lie at the heart of Sofra cuisine. Any rich sauces, which tend to obscure natural taste, are avoided. In assemblies, such as pilavs, pasta dishes and güveçs, ingredients are bound together with rice or bulgur, with yogurt or the natural juices of tomatoes or mushrooms. On their own, vegetables play an important role – reflected in Sofra's vegetarian restaurant award – but they are also used imaginatively to create a moist, steamy atmosphere in which other ingredients can be cooked. Where an unctuous cooking medium or dressing is demanded, first-class olive oil is used for its inimitable fruity taste, and its guarantee of no cholesterol.

Despite Turkish regional culinary differences, there exists a silver thread of commonly shared tendencies which I exploit when I create a new dish. For example, the use of yogurt is extended to healthy marinades (Chicken Breasts with Yogurt, Garlic and Coriander, page 51), and to sculpted desserts set with gelatine (Yogurt Ring Mould, page 120). The Turkish fondness for marrying sweet spice to savoury ingredients is the impulse behind new ways with monkfish, chicken and vegetable pilavs. The ancient affection for feta and walnuts is reconciled with modernity's demand for pasta (Pasta with Feta, page 107, and Pasta with Walnuts, page 102), and never is the food too fiery hot or heavily spiced. Chilli and paprika are used with discernment, the aim being not to mask the ingredients, but to lend them a clean, pungent edge.

I wanted this to be a practical book, which is actually used, every day, in a domestic setting. With this in mind, I have omitted a few of the Sofra restaurant recipes which are best left to professional production. In their place come recipes that I, and the chefs at Sofra, have either adapted from our menus or created specially for the home cook. With the exception of the İçli Köfte (page 12), none of the recipes are labour intensive; many can be made in advance. This ease of preparation is in fine Turkish tradition. It allows for relaxation, warm hospitality and the living of life to its fullest extent. It also ensures that what emerges from this book is a unique, eclectic cuisine with its finger firmly on the pulse of contemporary living.

Huseyin Ozer

Starters and Meze

Falafel

Over 3,000 years ago, a Hebrew cook, or perhaps an Egyptian one (who knows?) created falafel which, today, we might describe as a vegetarian rissole or fritter. Falafel have survived in Israel and Egypt and, additionally, radiated their influence throughout Turkey, Syria, Lebanon and Jordan. The fact that falafel are a rich source of protein, just as you would expect a bean rissole to be, may have contributed to their phenomenal success throughout the Middle East and Turkey. Yet, for the most part, their reputation is due to their taste, and to that all-important element of texture. Crisp to the point of crunch on the outside, tender and well-spiced within, falafel are irresistible.

There are certain national differences: in Israel and the Fertile Crescent, falafel are made with chick-peas, while in Egypt, where the rissoles are known as *ta'amia*, dried white broad beans – known variously as *ful nabed* and *fava* – are used. These are available from specialist shops and from most Turkish and Middle-eastern grocers. If possible, buy them without their skins, otherwise you will have to slip off the skins once they have been soaked.

At Sofra, we combine chick-peas with broad beans. And, in the tradition of the home-cook, we add more vegetables and green herbs to the mixture than would be found in the falafel of Middle-Eastern street stalls and cafés. The important thing is to make them how you like them, and call them your own.

Falafel

These illustrious, deep-fried little rissoles, so famous throughout the Middle East, are created from a fairly humble basis of either dried broad beans or chick-peas. The culinary status of the basic ingredients becomes elevated, however, once crucial flavourings are brought into play. Heady mixtures of aromatic vegetables, fresh coriander, cumin and mint lift the sturdy beans and chick-peas to dizzy heights of flavour. If you find dried broad beans difficult to obtain, just make the falafel entirely of chick-peas – which is the favoured method in Israel. Otherwise, try a mixture of the two, as here.

Serves 6–7 (makes 24–28 falafel)

Ingredients

225g/$^1/_2$ lb/1 cup dried chick-peas, soaked for 12 hours
200g/7oz/1 cup dried white broad beans, soaked for 12 hours
3 cloves of garlic, crushed
1–1$^1/_2$ teaspoons cumin
1 teaspoon ground coriander
$^1/_2$ teaspoon ground white pepper
salt
1 red pepper, deseeded and coarsely chopped
$^1/_2$ green pepper, deseeded and coarsely chopped
85g/3oz white part of leek, coarsely chopped
55g/2oz spring onion, coarsely chopped
$^1/_2$ Spanish onion, coarsely chopped
115g/4oz celery, destringed and finely chopped
70g/2$^1/_2$ oz/$^1/_3$ cup bulgur, soaked in boiling water for 15 minutes, then drained
4–5 tablespoons finely chopped fresh coriander or flat-leaf parsley
2 tablespoons finely chopped fresh mint

For frying
vegetable oil or ground nut oil
about 4 tablespoons flour (optional)

1 In a food processor, blend the chick-peas, broad beans, garlic, cumin, ground coriander and white pepper to an even, but slightly coarse, paste; transfer to a mixing bowl.

2 Put all the remaining ingredients into the food processor. Pulse them briefly, for just 5–8 seconds, or until they are extremely finely chopped but not yet a purée.

3 Using the food processor, blend the two mixtures together, in batches if necessary. Aim for a workable paste, with little pinheads of colour, which holds together when shaped into a ball. To achieve this,

3

you may need to add a few tablespoons of water. When the consistency is right, put the mixture in the refrigerator to rest for 30 minutes.

4 Divide and roll the mixture into 24–28 balls about the size of a walnut. You can keep the shapes as balls, which are best for deep-frying, or you can flatten them into patties, which lend themselves well to being shallow-fried. A third option is to mould them into pointed dome-shapes using a special falafel tool. When all the falafel are shaped, put them in the refrigerator to rest for 20 minutes.

5 Before frying an entire batch, try frying just one. If the mixture does not hold together, roll the falafel in flour. Deep-fry balls and dome-shapes for 6–8 minutes, or until crisp and deep golden-brown on the outside, with a cooked but tender inside. Alternatively, shallow-fry patties for 2–3 minutes on each side.

6 Remove from the oil and drain on kitchen paper briefly. Serve hot. Possible accompaniments include tomato – or tomato and cucumber – salad *(see page 19)*, yogurt scattered with fresh mint or coriander, cacık *(see page 14)* and warm pitta bread.

Chick-Pea Salad with Coriander

With their subtle, nutty taste, chick-peas are a wonderful foil for the sharp, tingling flavours of lemon juice, red onion and fresh coriander. If you use good-quality canned chick-peas, rinsed thoroughly of their brine, you can assemble the entire salad very quickly.

Serves 4–6

Ingredients

225g/½lb dried chick-peas, soaked, then cooked until tender OR
900g/2lb canned chick-peas, rinsed and drained
1 small red onion, finely chopped
½ cucumber, peeled, deseeded and coarsely chopped
juice of 1 large lemon
3 tablespoons olive oil
2 medium tomatoes, peeled and finely chopped
salt and freshly ground black pepper
7 tablespoons finely chopped fresh coriander

1 In a small bowl, combine the chick-peas, red onion, cucumber, lemon juice and olive oil. Mix well. Incorporate the tomatoes gently, so they retain their shape. Season well with salt and freshly ground black pepper.

2 Just before serving, stir in the fresh coriander. Serve with lots of crusty bread.

Patlıcan Salata

Although this can be loosely described as an aubergine salad, its appearance is certainly of a purée –
just as taramasalata looks like a purée. It lends itself to attractive decoration and to several different
accompaniments – it can be eaten with bread or with lettuce leaves, for example, or on sticks of
cucumber or celery. Once the aubergine flesh is softened by cooking, the puréeing process takes only a
matter of minutes. If you bake the aubergines over charcoal, as we do at Sofra, you will imbue their
flesh with an inimitable smoky flavour. Bear this in mind when you next have a barbecue.

Serves 2

Ingredients

1 large aubergine
1 tablespoon finely chopped red pepper
1 tablespoon finely chopped green pepper
1 clove of garlic, crushed to a pulp
a squeeze of lemon juice
a dash of white wine vinegar
salt and ground white pepper
olives to garnish
strips of red pepper to garnish
fresh dill to garnish

1 Slash the aubergine's skin with a knife in 9 or 10
places. Grill or roast it, turning occasionally, until
the skin has blistered, and the flesh feels soft when
poked. If you place the aubergine 2.5cm/1 inch from
the heat source of a hot oven grill, the process will
take 20–30 minutes. If you roast it in an oven
preheated to 240°C/475°F/gas mark 9, the process
will take 30–40 minutes.

2 When the aubergine is cooked, wrap it in a damp
kitchen towel. When the skin is cool, peel it away,
scraping off any flesh that clings.

3 Chop the flesh to a purée, gradually incorporating
the red and green pepper and the garlic. You can do
this in a blender if you wish; but the process is very
fast by hand as the flesh is so soft. Transfer the
mixture to a bowl. Stir in the lemon juice, the wine
vinegar and seasoning to taste. Set aside to cool
completely.

4 Spread the purée over a large serving plate. Garnish
with olives, strips of red pepper and fresh dill. Serve
with yogurt, pitta bread and lettuce leaves.

Patlıcan Kızartma

This attractive arrangement of fried aubergine, peppers, yogurt, paprika and fresh dill is the closest that Sofra cuisine comes to making pictures on plates. However, the arrangement does serve the purpose of keeping cool flavours distinct from hottish ones. In the restaurants, we prepare this dish using Charleston peppers. They look a bit like elongated chillies but they taste virtually as cool as sweet peppers, and their skins are deliciously thin and edible. The recipe works perfectly well without them, though. Just substitute sweet peppers or, if you crave something hotter, use mild chillies. The aubergines are sliced in a way that yields petal shapes. Long thin aubergines meet this aim best. The dish should be served at room temperature.

Serves 4

Ingredients

2 medium aubergines, each weighing 225–285g/8–10oz
salt
5 cloves of garlic, crushed to a pulp
340g/12oz/1$\frac{1}{2}$ cups natural yogurt
about 8 tablespoons vegetable oil for frying
EITHER
2 Charleston peppers, left whole
OR
4 mild chilli peppers, left whole
OR
$\frac{1}{2}$ green pepper, deseeded
30g/1oz butter, preferably clarified
1 teaspoon paprika
1$\frac{1}{2}$ tablespoons finely chopped fresh dill

1 Top and tail the aubergines. Partially peel them lengthwise to obtain alternating stripes of peel and flesh. Slice each aubergine across at 2cm/$\frac{3}{4}$-inch intervals, cutting diagonally at 45 degrees. Each aubergine should yield 8 petal-shaped slices and 2 offcuts from the ends. Immerse all the slices and offcuts in well-salted water, weighted down by a plate, for at least 20 minutes; this will remove any bitterness.

2 Meanwhile, mix the garlic and yogurt. If the yogurt looks too thick to spread smoothly, thin it with water.

3 Drain the slices of aubergine, wash them, drain again and dry on kitchen towels. Fry the slices (and offcuts) in a single layer, in batches, in shallow oil over a medium heat for 2–3 minutes on each side, or until golden brown. Add a little more oil with each batch as necessary. Drain on kitchen towels.

4 If using Charleston or chilli peppers, fry them whole in oil for several minutes. When they are cool, top and tail them, split them lengthwise and pick out their seeds, so that you obtain edible strips of pepper. Alternatively, grill half a green pepper until its skin blisters. Wrap it briefly in a cold, wet kitchen towel, then peel away the skin. Slice the half into 4 long strips. Set aside.

5 On each serving plate, arrange 4 long slices of aubergine to look like the petals of a flower. Put an offcut in the middle. Cover the vertical petals with a long line of yogurt. Cut the strips of pepper in half and lay half on each of the horizontal petals. Heat the butter. Drizzle it along the yogurt in a little stream, then scatter over some paprika. Sprinkle fresh dill over the horizontal arm. Serve at room temperature with bread.

Kısır

Kısır is quite probably one of the healthiest salads ever created. It is a loud, colourful pageant of all manner of nuts, soft-leaved herbs, vegetables and utterly exhilarating spices. I love it – flavours race across the palate with such speed and excitement that it is hard to pin down any single one; so you scoop another portion into a lettuce leaf or a piece of pitta bread, and eat some more. And you do this again, and again …

Serves 8

Ingredients

225g/8oz/1¹/₃ cups bulgur
55g/2oz/¹/₂ cup walnuts, coarsely chopped
85g/3oz/¹/₂ cup whole hazelnuts, coarsely chopped
1 tablespoon caster sugar
140g/5oz bunch of spring onions, very finely chopped
¹/₂ Spanish onion, very finely chopped
¹/₂ red pepper, deseeded and very finely chopped
¹/₂ green pepper, deseeded and very finely chopped
5 tablespoons finely chopped fresh flat-leaf parsley
4 tablespoons finely chopped fresh mint
5 tablespoons finely chopped fresh dill
1 teaspoon dried crushed chillies
1¹/₂ teaspoons paprika
1 teaspoon cumin
1 teaspoon ground white pepper
1 teaspoon freshly ground black pepper
175–200ml/6–7fl oz/³/₄ cup olive oil
5 tablespoons lemon juice
140–200ml/5–7fl oz/²/₃–³/₄ cup tomato juice
salt
a few wedges of lemon to garnish
a few slices of tomato to garnish
a few cos lettuce leaves to serve
pitta bread to serve

1 Put the bulgur in a large bowl. Pour over boiling water, and leave for 15 minutes. Drain in a fine sieve, rinse under cold water then drain again thoroughly, squeezing out the excess water with your hands. The bulgur should still have a firm bite at this stage.

2 In a large mixing bowl, combine all the dry ingredients listed, from the walnuts down to the black pepper. Add the well-drained bulgur. Mix well to distribute the ingredients evenly.

3 Stir in the oil, lemon juice, and as much of the tomato juice as you need to achieve a mixture that is moist and juicy without being over-wet. Taste, and season with salt and, if desired, more dried crushed chillies.

4 Leave the kısır to stand at room temperature for about 20 minutes. During this time, flavours will intermingle and the bulgur will continue to swell and absorb liquid.

5 Transfer the kısır to a large, flat serving dish. Garnish with wedges of lemon and slices of tomato. Offer cos lettuce leaves and little envelopes of pitta bread as accompaniments.

Zeytin Yağlı Bakla

In Turkey, we use broad beans in salads such as this one a good deal. Here, their tender texture is juxtaposed with the crunch of red pepper. Fresh broad beans, with their kernels so ravishingly bright, speak of all that is vibrant and good about natural food. It is a pity that their season is so short in the west. However, they freeze well, and, at Sofra, we frequently use the frozen version. We usually leave the skins intact, but take precautions to prevent toughness. Fresh coriander gives a vigorous burst of flavour to this salad, but you could replace it with chives or dill. When spring onions are in season, their white part, sliced into fine rings, makes a pleasant addition.

Serves 4

Ingredients

1.6kg/3$^1/_2$ lb fresh broad beans in their pods
OR
900g/2lb frozen broad beans
salt
2 cloves of garlic, crushed to a pulp or finely chopped
1 red pepper, deseeded and finely chopped
1$^1/_2$ tablespoons finely chopped fresh coriander
5 tablespoons olive oil
1 tablespoon lemon juice

1 If using fresh beans, remove them from their pods. If using frozen ones, wash them well and drain them. Put the beans into a deep saucepan and add enough cold, salted water to cover them by about 5cm/2 inches. Cover with a lid. Bring to the boil over a medium heat. Adjust the heat to maintain a simmer, and cook the beans until tender. This will take only 10 minutes for young fresh beans but up to 45 minutes for older or frozen ones.

2 Drain the beans in a large colander. Leave them to cool naturally. If cold water is used to accelerate cooling, it will toughen the skins.

3 Meanwhile, in a large bowl, combine the garlic, red pepper, coriander, olive oil and lemon juice. Add the cooled beans, and turn all the ingredients gently by hand, so as to mix well without breaking up the beans.

4 Serve the salad at room temperature and offer bread to accompany.

İçli Köfte

The acclaimed mixture of pounded bulgur and ground lamb, known loosely as köfte, has innumerable variants. One is stuffed, or içli, köfte, where an outer shell is created to enclose a filling. For this, two types of köfte mixture are required: an ultra-smooth one for the outer shell, and a medium-textured one, spiked with nuts and herbs, for the filling. A lot of mystique and folklore surrounds the assembly. Indeed, the potential of a bride was once judged by her talent for making a perfect içli köfte shell. Actually, the assembly is great fun. The requisite long finger of legend, to shape the shell, remains advantageous, but by no means obligatory. More important is the action: once a hole is poked in the ball of köfte paste, the action of the index finger inside the shell is a bit like the scouring of a saucepan.

Serves 4 (makes 16 içli köfte)
Ingredients

For the filling
15g/^{1}/$_2$ oz butter, diced
1 medium Spanish onion, finely chopped
1 red pepper, deseeded and finely chopped
1 green pepper, deseeded and finely chopped
55g/2oz/^{1}/$_2$ cup pine kernels
55g/2oz/^{1}/$_2$ cup walnut pieces, finely chopped
2 pinches cumin
285g/10oz minced lamb
salt and ground white pepper
2 tablespoons finely chopped fresh, flat-leaf parsley
2 tablespoons finely chopped fresh dill

For the shell
680g/1^1/$_2$ lb minced lamb
225g/^{1}/$_2$ lb bulgur, soaked in cold water for 20 minutes, then drained
1 teaspoon paprika
^{1}/$_2$ teaspoon cumin
a pinch of caster sugar
about ^{1}/$_2$ teacup water
about 3 tablespoons olive oil for moistening the hands

ground nut oil for deep-frying
1 lemon, cut into wedges, to serve

For the filling

1 Put the butter, onion, red and green pepper, pine kernels, walnuts and cumin into a large, heavy-based saucepan. Cover and place over a low heat. Stir after several minutes, then leave the ingredients to sweat slowly for 15–20 minutes, removing the lid and stirring frequently.

2 Stir in the minced lamb and a good pinch each of salt and white pepper. Cover, and cook the mixture gently for 15–20 minutes, or until done, stirring several times.
3 Drain the lamb mixture through a colander. Discard the excess liquid and transfer the mixture to a shallow dish. Set aside to cool.
4 When you are ready to use the filing, taste it and adjust the seasoning. Mix in the parsley and dill.

For the shell and the assembly

1 Put the lamb, bulgur, paprika, cumin, sugar, water and a good pinch of salt into the bowl of a food processor or a blender. Process the ingredients to a perfectly smooth, pliable paste, adding more water if necessary. Refrigerate the paste, covered, for at least 20 minutes.
2 When you are ready to assemble the köfte, put the olive oil into a small dish. Dip in your fingers and smear some of the oil across your palms. Divide the paste into 16 balls a little larger than a walnut.
3 Keeping your hands lightly oiled at all times, take one of the balls, and roll it briefly to smoothness

between both palms. Poke a deep indentation in the middle, then enlarge the hollow by turning your index finger rapidly inside, and pressing down gently as if you were cleaning the bottom of a pan. Draw the surrounding paste upwards to make a tallish cup. Fill it almost to the top with the lamb mixture, using a teaspoon. Close the top of the cup by drawing its rim together into a slightly pointed shape. Work the opposite end into a pointed shape to match. Set aside. Repeat this step until the batch of içli köfte is complete.

For the cooking

1 Heat the ground nut oil in a large deep pan or in a deep-fat fryer. Slide in the köfte and fry them for about 5 minutes or until they are lightly browned

and have risen to the surface. Drain well and serve with wedges of lemon.

Cacık

Yogurt, which is used widely in Turkish cuisine, is incorporated into many salads, the most well-known of which is surely cacık – a cool concoction of yogurt and cucumber, perfumed with mint. The concept of cacık is utterly simple but, nevertheless, a few tips are worth mentioning: it is best to avoid grating the cucumber, otherwise the cacık turns watery. There is no need to salt and drain the cucumber to prevent it weeping, unless you have either grated it, or intend making cacık hours in advance. At Sofra, we choose thin-skinned cucumbers and leave the skin intact for better flavour and brighter appearance. Garlic can be included, or not, as the case may be. Regards the mint, the dried version is preferable. This is because prolonged contact between yogurt and fresh mint will cause the mint to acquire a slightly bitter taste and a rather sad colour. Properly made, cacık is wonderful and much more than a starter. It is a crucial element of the meze table and a partner for all manner of stews, pilavs, kebabs and roasts.

Serves 6–8

Ingredients

1 large cucumber weighing about 500g/1lb 2oz, very finely chopped
3 tablespoons dried mint
about 2$^1/_2$ tablespoons olive oil
4 cloves of garlic, crushed to a pulp (optional)
600g/1lb 5oz natural yogurt
salt and ground white pepper
several pinches of dried, crushed chillies to garnish
a few sprigs of fresh dill to garnish

1 In a large mixing bowl, stir together the cucumber, the dried mint and one tablespoon of the olive oil. Stir in the garlic if desired.
2 Add the yogurt, stirring well. If the yogurt is very stiff, mix in a little water, a tablespoon at a time, to loosen it. Season to taste with salt and white pepper. Chill briefly.
3 To serve as a starter, transfer to individual serving bowls or plates. Garnish the centre of each with about half a teaspoon of the remaining olive oil, a pinch of dried, crushed chillies and a sprig of fresh dill. Serve it with bread. To present cacık as part of a meze table, or as an accompaniment, arrange it on a large serving plate and garnish it decoratively.

Special Stirred Eggs with Feta

This is a speciality dish which has proved incredibly popular. Essentially, it is a simple marriage of eggs and feta cheese, conducted briefly over heat. The secret of its appeal, however, lies in the way the ingredients are stirred and merged: the distinctive properties of the egg white and egg yolk are retained, while the feta, loosened by warmth, melds into the eggs. The result is a suave mixture that belies its simplicity. The natural salt flavour of the feta negates the need for additional salt and gives the eggs a mysterious edge of piquancy.

Serves 1–2

Ingredients

3 eggs
30g/1oz butter, or a mixture of butter and oil
115g/4oz feta cheese, cut into small dice
freshly ground black pepper

1 Break the eggs into a bowl, ensuring that the yolks do not break; set aside.
2 Heat the butter, or the mixture of butter and oil, in a frying pan. When it sizzles, add the feta and stir it around for 30 seconds or so.
3 Add the eggs, taking care not to break the yolk. After a few seconds, use the flat of a fork to push the white up and down the pan, then across it, avoiding the yolk. When the white is slightly fluffy and lightly cooked, stir the yolk around the pan and cook for a few seconds longer.
4 Transfer to a serving dish. Grind over some black pepper and eat the mixture when it has cooled slightly.

A Salad of Spinach, Feta, Walnut and Pear

This is a marvellous standby salad as its main ingredients are often already present in the kitchen. In an emergency, any lack of spinach could be made up with other salad leaves. The special interest of this salad, though, is the play between the sweetness of the spinach and pear, and the saltiness of the feta. The walnuts hold both elements in balance. There is no need to salt the salad. The feta does it for you.

Serves 4

Ingredients

1 large pear, preferably a comice
4–5 tablespoons walnut oil or olive oil
115g/4oz baby spinach leaves
140g/5oz/1 cup feta cheese, finely diced
85g/3oz/1 cup walnut pieces
freshly ground black pepper
1 teaspoon lemon juice

1 Peel the pear, cut it in half, and cut each half lengthwise into 8 long sticks, discarding the core. Toss the 16 sticks in a very small amount of the oil and set them aside briefly.
2 In a bowl, combine the spinach leaves, feta cheese and walnut pieces. Grind over some black pepper. Drizzle over the lemon juice, then the remaining oil. Toss well.
3 Distribute the tossed salad across 4 individual plates and, on each, arrange 4 of the sticks of pear in a star shape.

Chicory, Walnut and Orange Salad

One of the pleasures of this salad is the joy of eating an orange without any trace of pith and membrane. You should be able to remove virtually all the pith when you remove the peel. The way to do this is to hold an orange in one hand. Take a small, sharp knife in the other hand and insert it vertically into the peel. Then use a slight sawing motion to work round the orange so that the peel and pith fall away in a neat spiral.

Serves 4

Ingredients

2 large oranges
salt and freshly ground black pepper
3 medium heads of chicory, trimmed free of cores
about 5 tablespoons olive oil
30g/1oz/$^1/_4$ cup coarsely chopped walnuts
2 teaspoons lemon juice
8 walnut halves to garnish
1$^1/_2$ tablespoons finely chopped fresh dill to garnish

1 Cut away the peel and pith from the oranges. Cut through to the centre of each orange, slicing along each side of the dividing membranes, so that the orange segments fall away free of membrane and pith. When all the segments have been freed, squeeze the emptied skeletal membrane over a jug and catch the juice. Set aside about 3 tablespoons of the juice. Season the orange segments with salt and pepper, and set aside.

2 Separate the chicory leaves and put them in a large mixing bowl. Season with salt and lots of freshly ground black pepper. Drizzle over 3 tablespoons of the oil and scatter over the chopped walnuts. With your hands, gently turn the leaves to coat them evenly. Make a dressing by combining the lemon juice, the reserved orange juice and the remaining oil; season to taste.

3 Arrange the chicory leaves in a single layer, hollow-side up, on individual serving plates, ensuring an even distribution of walnuts. Nestle the orange segments into the hollows of the leaves. Drizzle the dressing over the oranges. Garnish with walnut halves and fresh dill, and serve straight away.

Tomato Salads

When tomatoes burst with flavour and fragrance derived from outdoor ripening, on the plant and in the sun, they have a special magic. In this country, we often have to accept greenhouse varieties of tomato which, in terms of flavour, fall short of the ideal. For salads, the solution is to employ herbs and first-class olive oil; but for the tomatoes to absorb these flavourings fully, they must first be peeled.

I peel the extra-large, or ridged, varieties of tomato in a slightly quirky way; I cut horizontally through the skin, so it falls away in a continuous spiral. I then use the skin, curled into flower shapes, for garnish.

I also like to exploit the versatility of the tomato salad. This means not only exploring the herbs which have an affinity with tomatoes but also varying the way the tomatoes are cut, sliced or chopped, so as to produce different effects and textures. It is always worth bearing in mind that the greater the number of cut surfaces, the greater the ability of the tomato to absorb surrounding flavourings, especially if the salad is tossed. It is generally a good idea to let tomatoes stand in their dressing, so they can soak it up, for about 20 minutes before they are served. Remember that even the smallest pinch of salt will draw water from a cut tomato and make the salad watery; so add salt just seconds before serving.

Tossed Tomato Salad

When tomatoes are cut into tiny slices and tossed, their cut surfaces have the chance to intermingle effectively with delicate mixtures of tender, fresh herbs. Basil is best when it sings solo.

Serves 1–2

Ingredients

1 extra large, ripe tomato
1 tablespoon chopped fresh herbs, such as chives, chervil, basil or flat-leaf parsley
OR
$1/2$ teaspoon dried oregano, or dried mixed herbs
1 tablespoon olive oil
freshly ground black pepper and salt

1 Trim the stalk-end of the tomato to level it; remove the skin. Cut the tomato in half, lengthwise, through the core. Trim away the core. Lie each half, cut-side down, with the stalk-end pointing away from you. Cut vertical slices. Give the tomato a 45-degree turn. Slice vertically into 3 or 4 sections to produce small crescent shapes; transfer to a bowl.
2 Add the herbs of your choice, the olive oil and the freshly ground black pepper. Just before serving, sprinkle with salt and toss again.

Tomato Salad Variations

Sofra Chopped Tomato Salad on Bread

This is usually enjoyed as an open sandwich – ideal for lunch on the run. It is prepared in exactly the same way as for the Tossed Tomato Salad, above, except that the tomato is sliced then chopped finely. After the salad has been tossed with herbs, it is eaten piled on to crusty bread. Some people like the bread to be rubbed with a piece of cut garlic first.

Tomato Salad, Faintly Hot

This is another variation on the Tossed Tomato Salad, above. You can either slice the tomato into crescent shapes (step 1), or chop it finely. Add to the tomato mixture a mild chilli pepper and half a small red onion, both chopped very finely. You can eat it on bread, or not, as you wish. Either way, the result is very tasty and faintly hot.

Sliced Tomato Salad with Oregano

For this salad, the tomatoes are sliced to produce fan shapes, which can then be made to stand up in a serving dish to give an elegant presentation. The dominant herb here is oregano, the warm, spicy scent of which has a marvellous affinity with tomatoes. When fresh oregano is unavailable, use the dried version combined with fresh dill or chives.

Serves 1–2

Ingredients

1 extra-large, ripe tomato
$^1/_2$ teaspoon chopped fresh oregano, or dried
1 tablespoon olive oil
1 teaspoon chopped fresh dill or chives (optional)
salt

1 Trim the stalk-end of the tomato to level it; remove the skin. Cut the tomato in half, lengthwise, through the core. Trim away the core. Lie each half, cut-side down, with the stalk-end to the right. Slice vertically.

2 Arrange the slices, in fans or in simple rows, standing up if you like, in a serving dish. Add the oregano, then drizzle over the olive oil. If desired scatter over some fresh dill or chives. Just before serving, sprinkle with salt.

Potato Salad

The sumak used in this dish is a Turkish speciality, a brownish-purple spice with a peppery taste and lemony edge. It is available in most Turkish, Greek and Middle Eastern food stores. If you encounter any difficulty in obtaining it, don't let it prevent you from making the following recipe because the other ingredients combine to make a great potato salad regardless. The potatoes can be skinned or not, just as you prefer.

Serves 2

Ingredients

1 large or 2 medium potatoes, boiled and cut into chunks
2 tablespoons olive oil
$1/2$ red pepper, deseeded and finely chopped
$1/2$ red onion, finely chopped
OR
1 tablespoon chopped fresh chives
a pinch of sumak (optional)
a pinch of cayenne pepper
2 tablespoons chopped, fresh coriander
salt

1 Mix the potatoes and oil together in a bowl. Add all the remaining ingredients, except for the salt, then mix to distribute them evenly. Finally, season the salad to taste with salt. Serve on its own or with a selection of other salads.

Hünkar Beğendi

Aubergines and cheese are well-known companions. Here they team up to form a moreish purée which is stroked on to warm pitta bread in the manner of humus and taramasalata. As well as being a starter in its own right, it is a 'must have' sauce for asparagus, and an accompaniment for a range of kebabs *(see pages 72–5)*, güveçs *(see pages 53 and 61–2)* and Albanian Liver *(see page 67)*.

Serves 4

Ingredients

2 large aubergines
30g/1oz butter
6 tablespoons flour
100g/3$^{1}/_{2}$ oz mild English Cheddar cheese, grated
2 pinches caster sugar
90ml/3fl oz/$^{1}/_{3}$ cup double cream
200ml/7fl oz/$^{3}/_{4}$ cup milk
salt and ground white pepper
1 tablespoon finely chopped fresh dill
a few sprigs of fresh mint to garnish
a few small diamonds of red pepper to garnish

1 Grill or roast the aubergines until their skins are charred and their flesh soft *(see steps 1 & 2, Patlıcan Salata, page 6)*.

2 On a wooden board, chop the aubergine flesh to form a purée, then transfer it to a bowl and set aside.

3 In a large saucepan, melt the butter over a medium heat. Stir in the flour to form a stiff roux. Add the grated cheese, the sugar and the double cream. With a metal balloon whisk, stir continuously until the ingredients are smoothly blended.

4 Add the aubergine flesh and whisk well. Gradually incorporate the milk, stirring with the whisk to avoid lumps. Taste, and season with salt and white pepper. Let the mixture bubble slightly for about 5 minutes or until the mixture has lost its floury taste. Remove from the heat and set aside to cool slightly.

5 To serve the Hünkar Beğendi as a starter, transfer it, warm, to individual plates. Scatter with dill and garnish with mint leaves at the side of the plate. Dot with a few diamonds of red pepper and serve it straight away with warm pitta bread.

Tabbouleh

This particular tabbouleh contains heaps of fresh flat-leaf parsley, quite a lot of mint, and a relatively small amount of bulgur (cracked wheat). The result is a tingling salad, with a taste so vibrant that it is guaranteed to restore vitality and awaken the tiredest of palates. The parsley will also provide a major boost of vitamin C.

Serves 2

Ingredients

2 tablespoons bulgur
a large bunch of flat-leaf parsley, coarsely chopped
6 large fresh mint leaves, finely chopped
$^1/_2$ red onion, finely chopped
a pinch of caster sugar
2 tablespoons olive oil
2 tablespoons fresh lemon juice
1 extra-large tomato, peeled and coarsely chopped
salt and ground white pepper

1 Put the bulgur in a small dish and cover with a teacup of tepid water; set aside so that the bulgar can soften slightly.
2 Meanwhile, assemble the remaining ingredients, except for the salt and pepper, in a large serving dish. Stir them around to distribute evenly.

3 Tip the bulgur, and a few drops of the water that clings to it, into the serving dish and stir everything around. Season to taste. Leave to stand for 25 minutes, during which time the bulgar will soften yet still retain a slight crunch. Serve.

Salad of Prawns and Mushrooms

This is a light, refreshing cold starter which opens the palate wide for richer things to follow. For maximum visual appeal, choose small, even-sized mushrooms. When sliced, the mushrooms should resemble the size and shape of the peeled prawns. To clean the mushrooms, which should also be very white and firm, either rapidly wash and dry them, or wipe them with a damp cloth. Do not stint on the lemon and fresh herbs – they add a vital tingle. The preparation is very easy – and most of it is done in advance.

Serves 4

Ingredients

1 medium clove of garlic, coarsely chopped
salt and freshly ground black pepper
2$\frac{1}{2}$ teaspoons dried thyme
finely grated zest and juice of $\frac{1}{2}$ lemon
4–5 tablespoons olive oil
250g/9oz small button mushrooms, cleaned and thinly sliced
285g/10oz cooked prawns in the shell
2$\frac{1}{2}$ tablespoons finely chopped fresh dill or flat-leaf parsley
4 sprigs watercress to garnish (optional)
4 wedges lemon to garnish (optional)

1 To make the marinade, crush the garlic with a pinch of salt to form a smooth paste, preferably using a pestle and mortar. Mix in the pepper, thyme, lemon zest and juice. Stir in the oil, mixing well.

2 Put the sliced mushrooms in a large bowl. Pour over the marinade, and gently turn the mushrooms with your hands to coat them. Taste and season, adding more oil and lemon juice if you wish. Cover the bowl with clingfilm and marinate in a cool place for 2–24 hours.

3 Reserve 4 whole prawns for garnish, and shell the rest. Add the shelled prawns and the dill, or parsley, to the mushrooms. Mix everything gently with your hands. Cover, and leave at room temperature for 30 minutes.

4 Transfer the salad to individual serving plates. Garnish each with a sprig of watercress, a whole reserved prawn and a lemon wedge, if desired. Serve immediately.

Sweet Pepper Salad with Feta

Once a sweet pepper is grilled or roasted, and relieved of its tight skin, it reveals the full sweetness of its underlying flesh. Here, the characteristic sweetness is juxtaposed with the salty piquancy of feta cheese. It is a good match. When you roast or grill the peppers, you can, if you like, thread them on to long skewers, to facilitate their being turned. Remember to grill until the skins are conspicuously blistered and charred, so that the peppers are really easy to peel. For this recipe, I cut the skinned peppers into wide strips – 8 per pepper – but some cooks prefer to leave them in halves or quarters.

Serves 4

Ingredients

5 large or 6 medium peppers of various colours
1 medium clove of garlic
a very small pinch of salt
freshly ground black pepper
1 tablespoon lemon juice
1 teaspoon clear honey
5–6 tablespoons virgin olive oil
3 tablespoons finely chopped mixed fresh herbs or dill
55g/2oz/^{1}/$_2$ cup feta cheese, diced
a few pinches of paprika

1 Leave the peppers whole and set them beneath a medium-hot grill. When the skin blisters, turn them. Continue until they are blistered and charred all over.

2 Remove from the grill and wrap in damp kitchen towels. After 5 minutes, unwrap one of the peppers. Peel off its skin, working over a plate to catch the juices. Cut it in half lengthwise. Remove the stem, seeds and membranes. If wished, cut into quarters or strips. Transfer to a dish. Repeat with the remaining peppers.

3 Crush the garlic with the salt to a smooth paste, preferably using a pestle and mortar. Add ground pepper and stir in the lemon juice, the honey, the oil, the juices from the peppers, and half the fresh herbs. Stir well and pour over the peppers. Cover, and transfer them to a cool place to marinate for up to 24 hours.

4 Bring the peppers to room temperature before you serve them. Arrange on individual plates with some feta cheese and a pinch of paprika in the centre. Scatter over the remaining fresh herbs and serve.

Vine Leaf Parcels

Dolma, or stuffed vine leaves, are a favourite all over the Middle East and there are countless variations. This version has a rice-based filling which includes pine kernels and sweet spice. So delicious is the filling that it can stand as a dish in its own right. It is certainly worth making in a large quantity. Vine leaves which have been preserved in brine are now available in almost every supermarket, and their treatment is dealt with in the recipe below. With fresh leaves, the treatment is slightly different: you will need to parboil them until they become very limp, then drain them, rinse them in cold water and drain them again.

Serves 8–10 (makes about 48 parcels)

Ingredients

For the filling
about 225ml/8fl oz/1 cup olive oil
2 Spanish onions, coarsely chopped
115g/4oz pine kernels
340g/12oz/1³/₄ cups Basmati rice, well washed and drained
about 500ml/18fl oz/2¹/₄cups water
salt and ground white pepper
1 teaspoon caster sugar
2 tablespoons dried mint
2 teaspoons allspice
4 tablespoons finely chopped fresh dill
4 tablespoons finely chopped fresh parsley

For the vine leaf parcels
about 55 preserved vine leaves (usually 1¹/₂–2 × 225g/8oz packs)
1 large potato, peeled and thickly sliced
2 lemons, thinly sliced
1 Spanish onion, coarsely chopped
juice of ¹/₂ lemon
about 285ml/10fl oz/1¹/₃ cups olive oil
425ml/15fl oz/2 cups water

1 To make the filling, heat the oil in a large, heavy-based saucepan. Add the onions and let them soften slightly over a low to medium heat for about 4 minutes. Stir in the pine kernels and cook for a further 4 minutes. Add the rice, stirring for a few minutes to coat the grains evenly.

2 Add the water, salt, pepper, sugar, dried mint and allspice. Stir well. Cover the pan and simmer for about 20 minutes or until the rice is soft, stirring from time to time, and adding more water if the mixture becomes dry before the rice is cooked.

3 Remove from the heat and stir in the fresh dill and parsley. When the mixture is cool, it is ready for use as a filling or as a dish in its own right. Covered in clingfilm and stored in the refrigerator, the filling will keep for up to a week.

4 For the dolma, soak the preserved vine leaves for about 15 minutes in several changes of cold water, unfolding them carefully as you work; drain.

5 Blanch the leaves in boiling water for about 3 minutes; drain, rinse in cold water, drain again and pat dry. Set any unevenly-shaped leaves to one side for later use in sealing the pan; you will need about 5 of these.

6 To prevent the dolma from sticking to the pan and burning, line the bottom of a large saucepan with a layer of the sliced potato. Put the slices of one of the lemons, together with the chopped onion, on top; set the pan aside.

7 To assemble the vine leaf parcels, take one of the leaves and lay it, vein-side up, on the outstretched palm of one hand. With the other hand, smooth the leaf, position its stalk-end near your wrist and nip off the stalk. Put a heaped teaspoon of the filling near the stalk-end. Fold over the sides of the leaf then roll it up to make a little parcel. Give it a gentle squeeze to make the ingredients cohere, then pat the sides to neaten them. Repeat the process until all the filling is used.

8 Place all the stuffed vine leaves side by side in the pan, packing them tightly in concentric circles. Top with a layer of the remaining lemon slices. Add the lemon juice, oil and water. Cover with the reserved leaves, avoiding gaps. To hold everything in place, put 2 plates, wrapped in foil, on top. Cover with a lid.

9 Set the pan over a medium heat. Bring the liquid to the boil, leave it to boil gently for 10 minutes, then adjust the heat and simmer for 35 minutes. Allow the dolma to cool in the pan. Remove the covering of plates, leaves and lemon slices. Serve the dolma tepid or cold.

Börek

Ready-made filo pastry, now widely available in supermarkets, is perfect for this recipe. It comes mostly in 275g/9$\frac{1}{2}$ oz boxed packs which contain 12 sheets, each about 23cm/9 inches × 25cm/10 inches. The bottom sheet, however, is often torn; so realistically, you wind up with 11. The good news is that they are of a perfect size for cutting the required strips, of 7.5cm/3 inches × 25cm/10 inches, for the börek. Just make two long cuts down a neat stack of filo sheets and your strips are instantly created. You will need a very sharp knife, though, and a ruler of some kind to ensure a straight edge. Each strip, when filled and folded, will produce a börek triangle. So easy is it that you will be able to complete an entire batch in minutes.

Serves 8–10 (makes about 33 triangular parcels)

Ingredients

500g/1lb 2oz feta cheese
100g/3$\frac{1}{2}$ oz finely shredded fresh spinach
2 eggs, the yolks separated from the whites
275g/9$\frac{1}{2}$ oz filo pastry
olive oil for frying

1 Crumble the feta into a bowl and work it to a smooth paste by hand. Add the spinach and the egg yolks, then knead until the ingredients are distributed evenly. Set this filling aside.

2 With a very sharp knife, cut the filo pastry into 7.5cm/3 inch × 25cm/10 inch strips.

3 Take one of the strips and lay it with its short edges directly facing you. Position a rounded teaspoon of the filling centrally, about 4cm/1$\frac{1}{2}$ inches from the short edge nearest to you. To enclose the filling and form a triangle, bring one corner diagonally across to the opposite side. Fold the triangle over itself, along the straight edge. Continue to fold the triangle across and over until you have a small flap of pastry remaining. Brush the flap with egg white and fold it over to seal the parcel. Repeat this step until all the filling is used.

4 Put enough olive oil into a pan to give a depth of about 4cm/1$\frac{1}{2}$ inches, then heat the oil over a medium heat. Dip the parcels briefly in cold water, then drop them – a few at a time – into the pan. Fry for 3 minutes, or until golden on both sides. Remove with a slotted spoon and drain on kitchen towels. Let the börek cool slightly before serving.

Börek

The term *börek* describes Turkey's glorious range of daintily-shaped pastries filled with savoury delicacies. The pastry dough employed can vary, as can the cooking method and the shape.

In Turkey, my mother excelled in country-style cooking and, during my childhood, she made wonderful Tartar börek: crisp, golden triangles, light as air, concealing a tender heart of melting cheese flecked with spinach or herbs. The pastry was made from *yufka* – dough rolled out paper-thin in the manner of French *mille feuille* and Greek *phyllo*, or filo. I remember the dough being difficult to handle.

Similar börek are a firm favourite with my Sofra restaurant clientele. Customers also find them a big success at parties at home because they make such ideal finger-food. Fortunately, everybody – even debutante cooks – can make them easily nowadays, thanks to commercially-made filo pastry which is available in virtually every supermarket. As well as being fabulous finger-food, and a must for the *meze* table, they also make an appetizing light lunch, served with salad.

Chilled Yogurt Soup

This is a refreshing soup which, like the salad Cacık *(see page 14)*, brings together a favourite trio: cucumber, yogurt and mint. The cucumber can be either finely chopped or grated depending on the sort of texture you want to give to the soup. I prefer the former, but it is all down to personal taste. For the mint, use the dried variety in the soup itself but fresh mint for the garnish. This sounds curious, I know, but yogurt will cause fresh mint to turn bitter if there is prolonged contact.

Serves 4

Ingredients

1 large cucumber weighing about 500g/1lb 2oz, any old, coarse skin peeled away
2 × 500g/1lb 2oz cartons natural yogurt
2 tablespoons dried mint
1 clove of garlic, crushed to a pulp (optional)
about 175ml/6fl oz/³/₄ cup water
salt and ground white pepper
4 sprigs fresh mint to garnish

1 Cut the cucumber in half, crosswise, then cut each half lengthwise into 3 long sections of flesh, avoiding the centre section of seeds. Discard the seed section. With a potato peeler, scrape off 4 long, thin strips of cucumber peel. Roll each into a little scroll and set aside for garnish. Finely chop or grate the sections of cucumber flesh.

2 Mix together the yogurt, dried mint and, if you like, the crushed garlic. Stir in the cucumber and enough water to produce the consistency of thin cream. Season to taste. Cover the mixture and chill it.

3 To serve, stir the soup well and ladle it into 4 individual bowls. Garnish each with a reserved scroll of cucumber and a small sprig of fresh mint.

Chilled Tomato and Cucumber Soup with Yogurt

Simplicity itself, this is a marvellous soup for summer when tomatoes are packed with flavour. A small tip though: when you sieve the puréed tomatoes, use a nylon sieve rather than a metal one which can sometimes spoil the flavour.

Serves 4

Ingredients

1.3kg/3lb tomatoes, peeled and coarsely chopped
2–2$\frac{1}{2}$ teaspoons caster sugar
140ml/5fl oz cold water
salt and ground white pepper
4$\frac{1}{2}$ tablespoons natural cow's milk yogurt (not the set variety)
about 6 tablespoons finely chopped cucumber
4 teaspoons finely chopped fresh dill or fresh mint to garnish

1 In a food processor or a blender, pulse the tomatoes to a smooth purée.

2 Over a bowl, rub the purée through a nylon sieve using the edge of a wooden spoon. Discard the seeds which remain in the sieve.

3 Stir the caster sugar and water into the purée; season to taste. Cover and chill.

4 Just before serving, stir in 3 tablespoons of the yogurt and all of the cucumber. Pour into 4 individual soup bowls. Garnish the centre of each with a blob of the remaining yogurt and some fresh dill or mint.

Main Course Vegetarian

Silk Route

This rapid sauté of a colourful spectrum of vegetables is indebted to China for several of its key ingredients. However, these pass through the kitchen conventions of the Middle East and Europe – a journey not unlike the spice and silk routes of the Middle Ages. Because the vibrant colour and soft sheen of the lightly cooked vegetables remind me of silk, I named the dish accordingly. The rapid sautéing method allows the vegetables to retain their crunch and healthy nutrients. And rapid it is! The whole thing takes 10 minutes.

Serves 2

Ingredients

3 tablespoons olive oil
2 cloves of garlic, finely chopped
1 small Chinese cabbage, sliced
8 small to medium button mushrooms, sliced
100g/3½ oz mangetout, topped and tailed
1 red pepper, deseeded and sliced
1 green pepper, deseeded and sliced
1 small (or ½ large) aubergine, peeled, halved lengthwise, then sliced across into fan shapes
1 tablespoon oyster sauce
1½ tablespoons light soy sauce
a pinch of ground nutmeg
1 teaspoon caster sugar
1½ tablespoons cornflour, mixed with 1 teacup of water
salt and ground white pepper

1 Heat the oil in a large sauté pan set over medium heat. Sauté the garlic for 20 seconds, then add all the vegetables. Stir well and sauté for 4 minutes.
2 Add the oyster sauce, soy sauce, nutmeg, sugar and cornflour mixture. Stir to blend. Season to taste. Stir again, then sauté for a further 5 minutes, or until the vegetables are cooked to your liking.
3 Serve Silk Route hot or tepid, on its own or with rice and yogurt. The dish, in smaller quantities, can also accompany a simple meat or fish main course.

Mushroom Sauté

Mushrooms, which so often play a supporting role in main course cookery, are allowed to take centre-stage in this dish. Their natural taste is respected wholeheartedly and not blurred with herbs and unnecessary refinements. This honest, minimalist approach works superbly well; but, of course, the mushrooms must be absolutely fresh, with pure, pinkish-white skins. Personally, I add no pepper to this dish, but you may wish to.

Serves 2

Ingredients
6 tablespoons olive oil
$^1/_2$ small Spanish onion, finely chopped
$^1/_2$ large red pepper, deseeded and cut into 1cm/$^1/_2$ inch squares
400g/14oz large button mushrooms, sliced
salt and freshly ground black pepper (optional)

1 Heat 4 tablespoons of the oil in a large sauté pan set over a low to medium heat. Sauté the onion for 3–4 minutes, then add the red pepper and sauté for a further 2 minutes.

2 Stir in the remaining oil. Add the mushrooms in 2 batches, mixing gently to integrate each batch. Season to taste, then sauté for a further 2 minutes.

3 To encourage the mushrooms to exude their juices, cover the pan with a lid or some foil. Cook for a further 4 minutes, removing the cover every now and then to stir everything around.

4 Remove from the heat and serve the sauté hot, or tepid, on its own or with rice or bulgur.

Green Lentil Casserole

High in protein, lentils are teamed here with hearty vegetables to create a robust, nourishing casserole. The dish makes particularly good comfort food in winter, and can be eaten on its own or with rice or bread. In summer, use fewer lentils and more tomatoes, and garnish with basil or marjoram – or whichever soft fresh herbs take your fancy.

Serves 6–8

Ingredients

800g/1lb 12oz/4 cups green lentils, picked clean of impurities and rinsed in several batches of cold water
salt
3 tablespoons olive oil
1 clove of garlic, finely chopped
1 medium Spanish onion, coarsely chopped
2 medium carrots, coarsely chopped
1 large red pepper, deseeded and coarsely chopped
1 large green pepper, deseeded and coarsely chopped
1 vegetable stock cube, finely crumbled
3 medium tomatoes, peeled and coarsely chopped
1 potato weighing about 225g/8oz, peeled and diced
$^1/_2$ teaspoon dried crushed chillies or chilli powder
ground white pepper

1 Put the lentils in a large saucepan with enough water to immerse them by 3.5cm/1$^1/_2$ inches. Add salt and bring to the boil over high heat, removing any scum. Cover, lower the heat and simmer for 30 minutes or until the lentils are tender, adding more water if necessary. Drain, rinse well and drain again.

2 Meanwhile, in a large saucepan, heat the oil over a low to medium heat. Add the garlic, onion and carrots, and sauté until the garlic and onion soften – about 5 minutes. Stir in the 2 peppers and the crumbled stock cube. Cook for 10 minutes or until the carrot is tender.

3 Add the tomatoes, stir everything around for several minutes, then add about 850ml/1$^1/_2$ pints of boiling water. Bring back to the boil over high heat, add the potato and chilli, then season to taste. Adjust the heat to maintain a very light boil until the potato is just cooked.

4 Stir in the cooked drained lentils; adjust seasoning. Cover, simmer gently for 5–10 minutes to intermingle the flavours, then serve.

Ladies' Fingers Stew

This colourful stew of bamiya, or okra, intermingled with tomatoes and peppers, is a classic in Turkey and the Middle East. Because of its shape and its pointed tips, okra is often referred to colloquially as ladies' fingers. The tips and caps must be trimmed away prior to cooking; but when you trim them be sure not to expose the seeds and sticky juices inside otherwise the okra will open wide and lose shape during cooking. The sticky texture is precisely what gives okra its acclaimed succulence and, also, what gives the sauce of the stew its velvety body. Although this dish is usually served hot, the method of stewing in oil allows the dish to be appetizing when served cold.

Serves 4

Ingredients

680g/1$\frac{1}{2}$ lb fresh young okra
1$\frac{1}{2}$ medium cloves of garlic, finely chopped
1 medium Spanish onion, finely chopped
$\frac{1}{2}$ tablespoon coriander seeds, finely crushed
175ml/6fl oz/$\frac{2}{3}$ cup olive oil
1 small red pepper, coarsely chopped
1 small green pepper, coarsely chopped
3 extra large tomatoes, peeled and coarsely chopped
1$\frac{1}{2}$ tablespoons tomato purée
$\frac{1}{2}$ teaspoon caster sugar
2 teaspoons dried crushed chillies
salt and ground white pepper
2 tablespoons lemon juice
1 tablespoon finely chopped fresh coriander to garnish

1 Wash and dry the okra. Cut off and discard the pointed tips and caps.
2 In a large saucepan, sauté the garlic, onion and crushed coriander seeds in the oil for 5 minutes. Stir in the red and green peppers and cook for a further 2 minutes.
3 Stir in the tomatoes and the okra. After a minute or so, stir in the tomato purée, sugar and dried chillies. Add enough water to just cover the ingredients. Season to taste. Bring to the boil, cover, then simmer for about 30 minutes or until the okra are just tender.
4 Add the lemon juice and cook for a further 5 minutes. Scatter with fresh coriander and serve.

Zeytin Yağlı Enginar

This elegant little stew brings together the compatible textures of artichoke hearts, potatoes and gently simmered aromatic vegetables. It is very easy on flavour – nothing too hot or challenging; and the artichokes, which quarrel with many herbs, sit comfortably with the garnish of dill. An altogether delightful affair.

Serves 2–3

Ingredients

6 globe artichokes
juice of 1 lemon for preparing the artichokes
$^1/_2$ lemon for preparing the artichokes
15g/$^1/_2$ oz butter
5 tablespoons vegetable oil
3 cloves of garlic, very finely chopped
1 large Spanish onion, finely chopped
1 small red pepper, deseeded and coarsely chopped
1 small green pepper, deseeded and coarsely chopped
3 medium tomatoes, peeled and coarsely chopped
400ml/14fl oz/1$^3/_4$ cups water
2 teaspoons caster sugar
salt and ground white pepper
565–680g/1$^1/_4$–1$^1/_2$ lb potatoes, cut into large dice
1–2 tablespoons finely chopped fresh dill

1 Cut through each raw artichoke, remove its heart and put it into water and lemon juice (see 'Extracting Artichoke Hearts for Cooking', page 39).
2 Heat the butter and 3 tablespoons of the oil in a large sauté pan or saucepan set over a low to medium heat. Sweat the garlic and onion, covered, for 5–8 minutes. Add the 2 peppers, sauté briefly, then cover the pan and sweat everything together for a further 3 minutes.
3 Drain the artichoke hearts and add them to the pan, hollow-side up. Drizzle over the remaining oil.

Sauté, uncovered, shaking the pan slightly for several minutes, then add the tomatoes and stir them around. Stir in the water, the sugar and seasoning to taste. Bring to a light boil, then cover and simmer for 20 minutes.
4 Add the potatoes, spoon over some juices, then cover and simmer gently for 15–20 minutes or until the hearts are tender and the potato is cooked. Just before serving, stir in fresh dill. Allow to cool slightly before transferring to individual serving plates.

Extracting Artichoke Hearts for Cooking

Although raw globe artichoke hearts can be bought, they are usually stored in a preservative of some kind and never taste the same as those that are prepared at home.

To extract the heart from a globe artichoke, start by cutting off the stalk and the lower two rows of leaves. Slice across the artichoke about two-thirds of the way down so that you are left with the bottom. Tug away whatever leaves you can. With a sharp knife, pare the artichoke bottoms starting at the point from which the stalk has been cut away, peeling spirally to remove all tough parts. The pared bottom, or heart, will resemble a small, greyish-green saucer containing some hairy choke which must be discarded.

To dislodge the choke, scrape hard with a sharp teaspoon or a vegetable ball-cutter. To prevent the heart from discolouring, rub it with half a lemon, then drop it into a bowl of cold water acidulated with the juice of one lemon.

What to do with the leaves of the artichoke? You can either discard them, or set aside the fleshiest ones to be cooked later and nibbled with melted butter as a dish in its own right.

Chick-Peas with Spinach and Tomatoes

This simple mixture, which can be put together in no time, brings together lively flavours and bright colours. The spices are racy rather than hot; and even though the coriander dominates the spice mixture, with its lovely hint of orange coming through, nothing detracts from the natural flavour of the basic ingredients. Although canned chick-peas can be used occasionally for certain dishes, I do not recommend them for this. Their flavour would not be conducive to the desired effect and their skins would fall off with cooking.

Serves 4

Ingredients

3–4 tablespoons olive oil
225g/8oz dried chick-peas, soaked according to packet instructions then simmered for about 1¼ hours, and drained
400g/14oz canned chopped tomatoes, drained of excess juice
2 extra-large tomatoes, peeled and cut into small even pieces
1 teaspoon cumin
1½ teaspoons ground coriander
1 teaspoon caster sugar
salt and freshly ground black pepper
375g/13oz spinach, washed

1 Heat the oil in a large saucepan. Add the chick-peas and shake the pan to coat them lightly in the oil. Stir in the canned tomatoes and the fresh chopped ones. Cover the pan and simmer for 3 minutes.

2 Remove the lid, raise the heat and stir until the fresh tomatoes have flopped yet retain some shape. Stir in the cumin, coriander, sugar and seasoning to taste.

3 Off the heat, add about two-thirds of the spinach, piling it on top of the chick-peas and tomatoes. Cover with a lid. Return to the heat and, after 2–3 minutes, when the spinach has flopped, push it down the saucepan and stir it into the other ingredients.

4 Stir in the remaining spinach. Cover and simmer for 2–3 minutes. Taste, adjust seasoning, and serve.

Sweet Spinach Flan with Raisins and Pine Kernels

Flans do not necessarily have to be set in a lining of pastry. For this one, where raisins and pine kernels reinforce the natural sweetness of spinach, I have used a thin lining of breadcrumbs to a lighter effect. The flan is cooked until just set, then left to firm up slightly during a brief resting period. If you use very young spinach with few tough stems, you will need up to 225g/¹/₂ lb less spinach than the quantity given below. It seems sensible to make a large flan, because it is so good cold and very versatile.

Serves 8

Ingredients

1.25kg/2lb 12oz fresh spinach, washed, tough stems removed (or 550g/1¹/₄ lb frozen chopped spinach)
salt
a little butter for lining the dish
3 tablespoons dry breadcrumbs
6 large eggs
450ml/16fl oz/2¹/₄ cups double cream
freshly ground black pepper
a good pinch of ground nutmeg
30g/1oz/¹/₄ cup pine kernels
2 tablespoons seedless raisins

1 Cook fresh spinach in plenty of boiling salted water for 1–2 minutes. Drain and refresh under cold water. Drain again and squeeze out moisture. Chop the spinach coarsely; set aside. (Cook frozen spinach according to packet instructions, then squeeze out moisture.)

2 Butter a flan dish 28cm/11 inches in diameter and sprinkle it with the breadcrumbs. Rotate the dish to coat it evenly; tap out the excess.

3 In a large bowl, beat together the eggs and cream. Stir in the spinach. Season with salt, pepper and nutmeg. Pour the mixture into the flan dish and scatter with the pine kernels and raisins.

4 Bake in an oven preheated to 180°C/350°F/gas mark 4 for 45–50 minutes or until lightly set.

5 Let the flan stand at room temperature for about 5 minutes before serving it cut into wedges.

Bean Feast

This is a glorious assembly of all kinds of dried beans. Be on your guard with the soaking and cooking times, which can vary drastically depending on the brand name. This is because drying processes are continually being improved; and it also explains why early cookery books mention 24 hours of soaking whereas the beans of today require nothing like that amount of time. Generally speaking, this is not a dish to make in small quantities. Ideally, have ready a large, flameproof casserole, attractive enough to put on the table.

Serves 8

Ingredients

170g/6oz/1 cup dried white haricot beans, soaked
115g/4oz/$^2/_3$ cup dried red kidney beans, soaked
140g/5oz/1 cup dried black-eye beans, soaked
75g/3oz/$^1/_2$ cup dried aduki beans, soaked
340g/12oz Spanish onion, coarsely chopped
30g/1oz unsalted butter
3 tablespoons olive oil
4 large garlic cloves, finely chopped
1.4 litres/2$^1/_2$ pints/6 cups passata
115g/4oz celery, destringed and thinly sliced crosswise
2 teaspoons dried thyme
2 teaspoons dried oregano
$^1/_2$ teaspoon dried crushed chillies
salt and ground white pepper
4 tablespoons finely chopped fresh coriander or flat-leaf parsley to garnish

1 Combine the white haricot and the red kidney beans in one large pan and combine the black-eye and aduki beans in another. Cover the beans in both pans with plenty of cold water – but no salt. Add lids to the pans and bring to the boil very slowly over the lowest heat. This will take up to 40 minutes.

2 Set the lids askew and simmer briskly for 10–15 minutes. Drain the beans, keeping their batches separate. Rinse in lots of cold water until the liquid runs clear; drain. Set the 2 batches of beans aside.

3 In a large sauté pan or saucepan, sweat the onion in the butter and oil for 10–15 minutes or until soft and translucent. Stir in the garlic, then the passata, and bring this tomato sauce to a simmer.

4 Transfer the sauce to an attractive flameproof casserole. Add the batch of white haricot and red

kidney beans. Cover with a lid askew and simmer for 35 minutes.

5 Add the batch of black-eye and aduki beans, along with the celery, dried thyme, oregano, chillies and seasoning to taste. Simmer for a further 30–40 minutes or until the beans are done to your taste.

6 Make a final adjustment to the seasoning, scatter with fresh herbs and serve.

Runner Bean and Tomato Stew

In this fine example of Turkish home cooking, runner beans, tomatoes and onions are packed, in alternating layers, into a deep saucepan, then steamed gently for about one hour. During this time, the runner beans absorb the surrounding cooking vapours and, in the process, acquire excellent flavour and sweetness. At the end of the cooking, the assembly is inverted onto a serving platter. Traditionally, some attractive vegetable shapes are arranged at the bottom of the saucepan so as to embellish the turned-out dish. In the absence of fresh runner beans, frozen ones or fine haricots verts can be substituted.

Serves 4

Ingredients

1 extra large Spanish onion or 1$^1/_2$ smaller ones, peeled
4 medium tomatoes
1.1kg/2$^1/_2$ lb fresh runner beans, topped, tailed, destringed and sliced vertically into 5cm/2 inch slices
OR
1kg/2lb 4oz sliced frozen runner beans
salt and ground white pepper
2 tablespoons caster sugar
125ml/4fl oz olive oil
about 900ml/2fl oz water

1 To create a decoration for the turned-out dish, cut a thickish slice from the top of the onion and place it in the middle of the base of a large saucepan, preferably about 11cm/4$^1/_2$ inches deep. Cut 2 large slices from one of the tomatoes. Cut the slices in half and arrange these 4 tomato 'fans' around the circle of onion. Coarsely chop the remainder of the onion. Skin and coarsely chop the remaining tomatoes.

2 Sprinkle over one-third of the chopped onion, then one-third of the chopped tomato, then one-third of the runner beans. Season with salt and white pepper. Repeat this layering process twice. Add the caster sugar, oil and enough cold water to almost cover the ingredients. Cover with a double layer of foil, ensuring a snug fit. Put a plate on top – one which fits just inside the saucepan – then cover with a lid.

3 Place the pan over medium heat and when, after about 10 minutes, the liquid comes to the boil, adjust the heat to maintain a low simmer. Continue to simmer until all the cooking liquid has been absorbed, checking after about 45 minutes. To check, remove the lid and plate, then slide a spoon down the side of the pan to see if liquid collects in the spoon's bowl, Depending on the thickness of the saucepan, the cooking time will vary from 45–90 minutes.

4 When the dish is cooked, remove its coverings, let it cool for 10 minutes, then invert the saucepan onto a large serving platter. Neaten the turned-out assembly and adjust its decoration if necessary. When the dish has cooled to room temperature, it is ready to serve.

Bulgur Pilav with Walnuts, Apricots and Aubergines

Although rice is the most common base for Turkish pilavs, bulgur is also a very popular choice. In this particular recipe, bulgur's slightly nutty edge is in perfect keeping with the walnuts, dried apricots, aubergine and cinnamon. What we have, in short, is a quintet of typically Turkish ingredients. Vegetarians will want to use vegetable stock or water for this pilav; non-vegetarians may prefer to include chicken stock.

Serves 4–6

Ingredients

140ml/5fl oz/^{2}/$_3$ cup olive oil
^{1}/$_2$ Spanish onion, coarsely chopped
1 medium aubergine, peeled and diced
1 medium red pepper, deseeded and coarsely chopped
115g/4oz/1 cup shelled walnuts, quartered or coarsely chopped
255g/9oz/1^1/$_4$ cups dried apricots, soaked according to packet instructions
85g/3oz/^{3}/$_4$ cup raisins
1 teaspoon ground cinnamon
565g/1^1/$_4$ lb/3^1/$_2$ cups bulgur, washed several times and drained
about 1.25 litres/2 pints/5 cups hot vegetable stock or boiling water
salt and ground white pepper
4 tablespoons finely chopped fresh dill

1 Heat the oil in a large deep-sided saucepan set over a low to medium heat. Sauté the onion until slightly soft. Add the aubergine, stirring to coat it evenly in the oil.

2 Cover the pan and, over low heat, sweat the ingredients, stirring occasionally, until the aubergine has acquired a light golden colour – about 12 minutes.

3 Stir in the red pepper, then the walnuts, dried apricots, raisins and cinnamon. Mix in the bulgur and the hot stock or water. Bring everything to the boil, then lower the heat, season to taste and cover the pan.

4 Simmer gently for 15–20 minutes or until the liquid has been absorbed and the bulgur is plump and tender.

5 Let the pilav rest in a warm place for 10 minutes. Fluff it up with a fork and mix in the fresh dill. Adjust seasoning, adding more cinnamon if wished, then serve.

Bademli Pilav

A good pilav, like this one which combines rice with whole roasted almonds and pistachios, should be light, fluffy, and so moist that it glistens. The handling of the rice *(see 'Preparing Rice', page 47*, simple though it may be, is crucial to success. In this instance, the almonds are best coloured in the oven, rather than sautéed in oil, the effects of which are too cloying for the intended purity of the pilav. This dish, which is a wonderful restorative for a jaded palate, can be offered as a light main course, or as an accompaniment for kebabs, güveçs (casseroles), sautés and grills.

Serves 4

Ingredients

455g/1lb/2¹/₄ cups Basmati rice, well-washed and drained
55g/2oz butter
2 tablespoons vegetable oil
about 850ml/1¹/₂ pints/3³/₄ cups boiling water
salt
85g/3oz/¹/₂ cup whole almonds, blanched
55g/2oz/¹/₂ cup pistachio nuts
2–3 tablespoons finely chopped fresh dill or flat-leaf parsley

1 Soak the washed and drained rice in warm water for 10 minutes; drain, wash and drain again.

2 Heat the butter and oil in a deep saucepan set over a medium heat. Add the rice and stir around to coat the grains. Stir in the boiling water and salt to taste. Simmer the rice, covered, for about 10 minutes, stirring occasionally. When the water has evaporated, leaving holes in the surface of the rice, the rice will be done.

3 Put a cloth beneath the lid of the saucepan. Leave the rice to rest in a warm place for 15 minutes.

4 Meanwhile, spread out the almonds on a baking sheet and roast them in an oven preheated to 200°C/400°F/gas mark 6 for about 8 minutes or until golden-brown. Add the pistachios for the last couple of minutes.

5 Fork up the rice, add the nuts and the fresh herbs, mixing quickly with the fork. Serve straight away.

Preparing Rice

The secret of a good pilav lies not only in the quality of the rice, which should be a long-grain variety, but, also, in its being washed properly. In Turkey, I would use boldo rice which has a fairly large grain and unsurpassed flavour and whiteness. Here, I find that Basmati rice makes a good substitute.

Of course, both the quality and the processing of rice varies a lot from one manufacturer to another. Often some trial and error is required to find a brand that suits. As a general rule, however, so-called 'washed' rice is rarely washed to the point of having all its starch removed; and it is the removal of the starch that helps to ensure that a pilav has the desirable qualities of lightness, fluffiness, moistness and separated grains.

I almost always find that I need to wash and drain rice several times. This step, along with the final step of resting the rice after cooking, makes sure that the grains are perfect.

Casseroles and Sautés

Chicken Casserole with Tomatoes, Honey, Spice and Almonds

Once you have placed this chicken casserole in a low oven, you can forget about it for the next 2 hours. At the end of the cooking, have ready the sautéed almonds and toasted sesame seeds. The almonds are best sautéed quickly in a tablespoon of oil in a frying pan, for 30 seconds on each side. The best way to handle the fly-away sesame seeds is to put them in a non-stick frying pan and shake them very gently over heat for about 1 minute. This nutty garnish balances the sweet flavourings of the honey and tomato sauce, and makes a significant difference to the taste – and appearance – of the finished dish.

Serves 4

Ingredients

salt and ground white pepper
4 large leg portions of chicken, to include thigh and drumstick and weighing about 1kg/2lb 4oz
$^{1}/_{4}$ teaspoon saffron threads, crushed to a powder
900g/2lb tomatoes, peeled and coarsely chopped
$^{1}/_{2}$ medium onion, very finely chopped or grated
1 teaspoon grated or chopped fresh ginger root
55g/2oz butter, diced
about 3 tablespoons thin honey
$^{1}/_{2}$ teaspoon ground cinnamon
55g/2oz/$^{1}/_{2}$ cup blanched, whole almonds, sautéed briefly in about 1 tablespoon groundnut oil
2 teaspoons sesame seeds, toasted

1 Season the leg portions generously and rub the saffron into their skin. Arrange in a single layer in a deep casserole. Add the tomatoes, onion, ginger and butter.

2 Cover with a lid and transfer to an oven preheated to 240°C/475°F/gas mark 9. After 10 minutes, reduce the heat to 180°C/350°F/gas mark 4. Cook the casserole for about 2 hours, testing for doneness after 1$^{1}/_{2}$ hours.

3 Remove the chicken portions and transfer them to a clean, covered casserole; set aside. Return the original casserole to a very high heat and boil the tomatoes rapidly for about 10 minutes or until they have reduced to a syrupy consistency.

4 Remove the tomato sauce from the heat. Stir in the honey and cinnamon; season to taste. Pour the sauce over the chicken. Cover the casserole and either simmer it on top of the stove or put it in a medium oven for a few minutes, so that ingredients can heat through and flavours can intermingle. Just before serving, scatter with the almonds and sesame seeds.

Chicken Breasts with Yogurt, Garlic and Coriander

One of the most valuable contributions that Turkish cookery has made to today's trend towards healthier eating is its tradition of yogurt-based marinades. In recipes such as this one, the enzymes in the yogurt help to tenderize the chicken breasts and keep them succulent without the need for additional fat. Here, the yogurt also carries flavouring of garlic, coriander and lime into the chicken to give it a pungent yet clean taste. Although this dish is cooked in the oven, I recommend it also for the charcoal grill or barbecue.

Serves 4

Ingredients

4 breasts of chicken, skinned
salt
1 tablespoon lime juice
finely grated zest of 1 lime
255g/9oz natural yogurt
3 cloves of garlic, crushed to a pulp
$^1/_2$ teaspoon ground ginger
1$^1/_2$ teaspoons ground coriander
1 teaspoon ground cumin
1$^1/_2$ tablespoons finely chopped fresh coriander to garnish
4 wedges lime to garnish

1 On the curved side of the chicken breasts, make 3 or 4 shallow diagonal slashes with a sharp knife. Rub the chicken with the salt and the lime juice.

2 In a large bowl, make the marinade by mixing together the zest of lime, the yogurt, garlic, ginger, coriander and cumin. Brush this over the breasts, working it into the slashes. Marinate the chicken in the mixture for at least 4 hours, preferably overnight.

3 Arrange the breasts in a single layer in a shallow ovenproof dish. Cover the dish with foil and bake in an oven preheated to 190°C/375°F/gas mark 5 for 25 minutes or until the chicken is done.

4 Garnish with fresh coriander and wedges of lime, then serve.

Chicken Sauté with Sweet Peppers

Some of the best things are the simplest. This is one of them: a one-pan sauté where chicken's unassertive flavour melds effortlessly with sweet peppers and where an integral sauce forms in the pan with virtually no help from the cook. The large leg portions of chicken which I use combine thigh and drumstick. Two of these – three at the very most – are all that an average 25cm/10 inch sauté pan will accommodate comfortably when making this dish, because space is needed for the peppers and for turning the legs. The dish feeds two hungry people. For four daintier appetites, divide the portions at the end of cooking. You can use peppers of any colour. I use orange and yellow. These retain a striking glow even when cooked.

Serves 2–4

Ingredients

30g/1oz butter
2 tablespoons olive oil
salt and ground white pepper
2 large leg portions of chicken to include thigh and drumstick and weighing about 500g/1lb 2oz
several pinches of allspice
about 2 teaspoons dried marjoram
200ml/7fl oz white wine
1/2 teaspoon caster sugar
2 large peppers of any colour, grilled, skinned and cut into strips *(see steps 1 & 2, page 25, Sweet Pepper Salad with Feta)*
2 teaspoons finely chopped fresh marjoram, or coriander or flat-leaf parsley
2–4 wedges of lemon to garnish

1 Heat the butter and oil in a large sauté pan with a lid. Season the chicken leg portions, then sauté them, uncovered, for 8–10 minutes, turning them frequently and sprinkling both sides with a good pinch of allspice and the dried marjoram.

2 Strain off excess fat from the pan. Add the wine and let it bubble for several minutes, scraping up the crusty bits from the bottom of the pan, and stirring to dissolve them into a sauce.

3 Add the sugar and the peppers. Stir everything around for a minute or two. Cover the pan with a lid and simmer gently over low heat, using a special mat if necessary, for about 30 minutes, testing for doneness after 25 minutes.

4 Transfer to serving plates. Scatter with the fresh herbs and garnish with lemon. Serve with rice and a green vegetable, such as spinach or mangetout.

Chicken Güveç

This simple chicken casserole is cooked chiefly in its own juices. These come from the use of succulent leg meat and from the various surrounding vegetables. Just a small amount of butter is required initially to protect the leg meat from drying out until its own juices start to flow. It is perfectly possible to replace leg meat with breast meat, but you would need to employ more butter or oil as a cooking medium.

Serves 3–4

Ingredients

30g/1oz butter
about 455g/1 lb boneless leg meat taken from 3 legs, trimmed of skin, and cut into 2cm/1 inch pieces
1 Spanish onion, coarsely chopped
1 small clove of garlic, finely chopped
1 small red pepper, deseeded and coarsely chopped
1 small green pepper, deseeded and coarsely chopped
170g/6oz button mushrooms, sliced
1 extra-large tomato or 2 smaller ones, peeled and coarsely chopped
a pinch of paprika
a pinch of chilli powder (optional)
salt and ground white pepper
2 teaspoons finely chopped fresh coriander or marjoram

1 Melt the butter in a heavy-based flameproof casserole or a large sauté pan, set over a low to medium heat. Add the chicken, stir well, then cover with a lid. Leave the chicken to cook fairly slowly for 10 minutes, adjusting the heat if necessary. Remove the lid occasionally to stir the chicken and to check that it is not cooking too quickly.

2 Add the onion, garlic and peppers. Stir to combine for 2 minutes. Cover and cook for a further 5 minutes or until the onion softens.

3 Add the mushrooms, stirring to incorporate them. Cover and cook for 4 minutes or until the mushrooms have exuded their juices. Add the tomato, paprika and chilli if desired. Season to taste. Cover and leave to simmer gently for a further 10–15 minutes.

4 Just before serving stir in the fresh herbs. Serve with a rice or bulgur pilav.

Yellow Chicken with Yellow Peppers and Saffron Pilav

This is an alluring way to bring colour and flavour to a steamed chicken which can otherwise look rather sullen. A mixture of saffron, spice and butter is slipped beneath the chicken skin and, also, painted over the surface. Yellow peppers, grilled and skinned, form a cheerful garnish. Sometimes, I put slivers of them beneath the skin too. You will need stock for this dish. In the absence of home-made stock, substitute a cube but use only one cube for every 2.3 litres/4 pints of water. Regards accompaniments, the choice is wide. I opt for the upbeat Saffron Pilav *(see page 56)*; but a Bademli Pilav *(see page 46)*, or any pilav, would be agreeable.

Serves 4

Ingredients

$^1/_2$ Spanish onion
3 cloves
about 2.3 litres/4 pints chicken stock
1 teaspoon saffron threads
a pinch of turmeric
a pinch of allspice
a pinch of ground nutmeg
salt and ground white pepper
55g/2oz softened butter
1 × 1.5–1.7kg/3lb 5oz–3lb 12 oz chicken without giblets
115g/4oz ready-to-eat dried apricots
2 large yellow peppers, halved, grilled and skinned *(see step 5, page 95, Red Mullet in Boats of Yellow Pepper)*
Saffron Pilav *(see page 56)* to serve

1 Remove the rack from a large steamer and, in the bottom, put the half of onion stuck with the cloves. Add the rack and enough stock to just reach the rack. Heat to simmering point.
2 Meanwhile, pound the saffron threads to powder with a pestle and mortar. Add the turmeric, allspice, nutmeg and seasoning, then combine with the butter. Smear a little of the spiced butter around the bird's cavity, and pack in the apricots.

3 At the neck end, slip your fingers carefully beneath the skin and wriggle them gently to loosen the skin of the breast and thighs. Slide two-thirds of the remaining spiced butter under the skin, covering the breast and as much of the thighs as you can safely reach without snagging the skin. Wipe the remainder over the outside of the bird, saving just a little to coat a piece of foil. Wrap the foil over the breast. Secure the neck flap and drumsticks.

4 When the stock simmers, put the chicken on the rack. Cover and steam very gently for about 1³/₄ hours, adding the halves of skinned peppers to the rack after 1 hour, and testing for doneness after 1¹/₄ hours.

5 When the chicken is done, transfer it to a serving dish; discard the foil. Strain the stock. Slice the peppers into slivers; drape some over the breast, the rest around it. Carve the bird at table, serving some of the apricots with each portion, along with the peppers, the strained stock and Saffron Pilav *(see page 56)*.

Saffron Pilav (accompaniment for Yellow Chicken with Yellow Peppers)

Rice, delicately flavoured and coloured with saffron, is something of a luxury, but so enticing; and here its slight honey flavour is enhanced by hints of cinnamon and clove. Connoisseurs of saffron will appreciate that, with recipes, it is always difficult to suggest precise quantities because saffron's concentration and quality varies greatly, depending on the producer. Powdered saffron, which comes in tiny cellophane packets, is very strong and you would need just two of these packets for the following recipe. Increasingly, saffron is packaged as threads. As a rough guide, about one teaspoon of threads, once crushed, will yield about half a teaspoon of powder. You can use a pestle and mortar or a rolling pin to do the crushing.

Serves 4

Ingredients

30g/1oz unsalted butter
about 1 tablespoon olive oil
225g/½ lb/1¼ cups Basmati rice, washed
500ml/18fl oz/2¼ cups water
salt
a little less than ½ teaspoon powdered saffron
2 whole cloves
1 stick of cinnamon
2 bay leaves
ground white pepper

1 In a large saucepan, heat the butter and oil. Stir in the rice and, when the grains are coated, add the water and a little salt. Bring to a light boil, uncovered. Add the saffron, stir once, then add the flavourings of clove, cinnamon and bay.
2 Adjust the heat, with the lid set slightly askew, to maintain a gentle simmer. Cook for about 15 minutes or until the liquid is absorbed and the rice tender.
3 Remove the flavourings. Add pepper to taste. Transfer the rice to a warmed serving dish, fluffing it up slightly with a fork.

Sultan's Crowns

This is a festive-looking dish where lightly-spiced morsels of lamb arrive looking like gift-wrapped parcels! Slices of aubergine and leaves of spinach form a decorative wrapping for the meat, while sealing in flavour and succulence. The assembled parcels can be prepared in advance ready for a final blast in the oven. A tomato-based sauce completes the dish. Choose either the simple one given here *(step 8)* or the more complex Spicy Tomato and Sweet Pepper Sauce *(see page 59)*. An impressive, but easy, presentation for a dinner party.

Serves 4

Ingredients

3 medium or 4 smaller aubergines, preferably long and thin
salt
30g/1oz butter
800g/1lb 12oz lean stewing lamb, cut into 2.5cm/1 inch cubes
$^1/_2$ large Spanish onion, coarsely chopped
$^1/_2$ red or green pepper, deseeded and coarsely chopped
225g/$^1/_2$ lb button mushrooms, sliced
$^1/_2$ teaspoon mild chilli powder
2 teaspoons paprika
ground white pepper
1 chicken stock cube, finely crumbled
2 large tomatoes, peeled and coarsely chopped
up to 8 tablespoons vegetable oil for frying
8 medium spinach leaves, stems removed
4 slices of peeled tomato to garnish
4 small pieces of green pepper to garnish
4 toothpicks
1 tablespoon cornflour
1 tablespoon tomato purée
1 teaspoon dried oregano
about 340 ml/12fl oz/1$^1/_2$ cups hot water

1 Cut the tops from the aubergines and partially peel them, lengthwise, to achieve alternating stripes of peel and flesh. Slice them lengthwise to obtain 16 very long slices about 1cm/$^1/_2$ inch thick. Immerse them in a bowl of well-salted water, weighting them down with a plate, for at least 20 minutes to remove any bitterness.

2 Melt the butter in a large sauté pan or saucepan set over a medium heat. Add the lamb and sauté it for about 5 minutes or until juices run and the meat is

57

lightly coloured on all sides. Remove the lamb and set aside.

3 Lower the heat slightly and sauté the onion and red or green pepper for about 8 minutes or until the onion is soft but not coloured.

4 Stir in the mushrooms and, when their juices run, return the meat to the pan. Add the chilli powder, paprika, white pepper, crumbled stock cube and tomatoes, stirring after each addition. Cook, uncovered, for about 18 minutes or until the tomatoes have broken down and the lamb is lightly cooked. If, during this time, the mixture looks dry, stir in a little water.

5 While the lamb simmers, drain the slices of aubergine, wash them, drain again and pat dry on kitchen towels. Heat 5–6 tablespoons of the oil in a frying pan over a medium heat. Fry the slices in a single layer, in batches, for 2–3 minutes on each side; add a little more oil with each batch as necessary. Drain on kitchen towels.

6 When the lamb is done, let it cool slightly, then adjust seasoning. Have ready a roasting dish large enough to contain 4 parcels of the lamb in a single layer.

7 To assemble a parcel, take 4 slices of the fried aubergine and, in the roasting dish, arrange the slices in a criss-cross, using 2 slices vertically and 2 horizontally. The slices should overlap at the centre of the cross shape by about 5cm/2 inches. Cover the centre with 2 spinach leaves, overlapping them slightly, and nestle one quarter of the lamb mixture into the leaves. Fold over the aubergine slices to make a parcel. Top with a slice of tomato and then a small piece of pepper; secure all with a toothpick. Repeat the process to assemble 3 more parcels.

8 For the simple tomato sauce, mix the cornflour, in a cup, with just enough cold water to form a smooth paste. In a jug, combine the tomato purée, dried oregano and the hot water, stirring until smooth. Whisk in the cornflour mixture, and pour the sauce over the parcels.

9 Bake in an oven preheated to 190°C/375°F/gas mark 5 for 10–15 minutes or until the spinach has wilted and the garnish topping has cooked through.

Spicy Tomato and Sweet Pepper Sauce

This is a hot – but not fiery – tomato sauce of concentrated flavour, full body and interesting texture. Versatile in the extreme, it will enliven a range of simple meat, poultry, fish and vegetable dishes; and it is in its element beside the barbecue. It keeps and reheats with great success, and is well worth making in a large quantity for freezing.

Serves 4–6

Ingredients

4 × 400g/14oz cans tomatoes, drained of excess liquid
5 tablespoons olive oil
1 Spanish onion, finely chopped
1 large clove of garlic, finely chopped
1 green pepper, deseeded and cut into small, even-sized pieces
1–2 green chilli peppers, deseeded and finely chopped
$1/4$ teaspoon hot chilli powder
1 tablespoon caster sugar
2 teaspoons mustard
2 teaspoons lemon juice
salt and freshly ground black pepper
3 tablespoons finely chopped fresh flat-leaf parsley or fresh coriander

1 Push the canned tomatoes through a nylon sieve set over a bowl, pushing with the edge of a wooden spoon. Discard the seeds and solids that collect in the sieve. Set the purée aside.

2 Heat the oil in a heavy-based saucepan and sweat the onion until soft but not coloured. Add the garlic and green pepper and stir for 1–2 minutes. Add the chilli peppers, the reserved tomato purée, the chilli powder, sugar, mustard and lemon juice. Bring to a boil, then adjust the heat and simmer briskly, uncovered, for 20–30 minutes, stirring occasionally.

3 Season the sauce to taste, and continue to simmer until the sauce has reduced to a consistency that will coat the back of a wooden spoon. Just before serving, stir in the parsley or coriander.

Quick Lamb Casserole

This gently spiced lamb casserole, crammed with colourful peppers, onions and sun-ripened tomatoes, is typical of family cooking at home in Turkey. It can be simmered effortlessly either on top of the stove or in the oven. It does well whether it is cooked rapidly or slowly, so that it will always accommodate your particular needs. It also reheats extremely well. The middle-neck fillet of lamb which is called for is widely available in supermarkets. If you do not see it in the fresh meat department, try the frozen counter.

Serves 4–6

Ingredients

40g/1$\frac{1}{2}$ oz butter, diced
1kg/2lb 4oz middle-neck fillet of lamb halved lengthwise, then cut crosswise into 2.5–4cm/1–1$\frac{1}{2}$ inch pieces
1 Spanish onion, coarsely chopped
1 red pepper, deseeded and coarsely chopped
1 green pepper, deseeded and coarsely chopped
5 tablespoons tomato purée
2 extra-large tomatoes, peeled and coarsely chopped
1 teaspoon paprika
about 225ml/8fl oz/1 cup hot water
salt and ground white pepper
1$\frac{1}{2}$ tablespoons finely chopped fresh coriander or flat-leaf parsley, or a few torn basil leaves

1   Scatter the butter over the bottom of a large, heavy-based, flameproof casserole. Add the lamb, then the onion and peppers. Cover, and set over medium heat for 5 minutes. Stir, lower the heat and cook for a further 7 minutes or until the onion is soft but not coloured.

2   Stir in the tomato purée, the tomatoes, paprika and hot water, then bring the liquid to the boil. Season lightly and cover with a lid.

3   Simmer the casserole gently or briskly to suit your requirements. As a guide, it will take about 30 minutes simmering fairly gently on top of the stove or in an oven preheated to 180°C/350°F/gas mark 4.

4   Before serving, adjust the seasoning and scatter with fresh herbs. Serve with a pilav or some plain pasta, and salad.

Lamb Güveç

This casserole of lamb includes mushrooms as well as the more usual aromatic vegetables and peppers. The juices which the mushrooms exude become part of the integral sauce. This is a very easy, good-natured dish which can be tailored to suit your taste buds as well as your working schedule. It lends itself well to the racy hot taste of chilli and paprika, yet it tastes complete with just a lingering hint of oregano. It can be simmered on top of the stove as here, or cooked at a more leisurely pace in the oven.

Serves 4

Ingredients

30g/1oz butter
565g/1lb 4oz middle-neck fillet of lamb, cut into small pieces
1 Spanish onion, coarsely chopped
1 small red pepper, deseeded and cut into 1cm/¹/₂ inch pieces
1 small green pepper, deseeded and cut into 1cm/¹/₂ inch pieces
170g/6oz button mushrooms, sliced
1 extra-large tomato, peeled and coarsely chopped
a pinch of paprika
1 teaspoon dried crushed chilli (optional)
salt and ground white pepper
¹/₂ teaspoon finely chopped fresh or dried oregano

1 Melt the butter in a heavy-based flameproof casserole, or a large sauté pan, set over medium heat. Add the lamb, stir well, then cover with a lid. Cook for about 8 minutes, removing the lid occasionally to stir the meat.

2 Adjust the heat to low. Add the onions and peppers. Stir for 2 minutes uncovered, then cover and cook for a further 5 minutes or until the onion softens.

3 Add the mushrooms, stirring well to incorporate them. Cover and cook for 4 minutes or until the mushrooms have exuded their juices. Add the tomato, paprika, chilli if desired and salt and pepper.

4 Simmer for a further 10 minutes on top of the stove or transfer to a preheated, slow to medium oven for 30 minutes or until done to your liking.

5 Just before serving, stir in the oregano.

Kidney Güveç

This is one of the best treatments for kidneys that I know. The kidneys emerge succulent, light and clean-tasting, unmuddied by the kind of heavy clinging sauces usually associated with them. Although kidneys have a potentially dominant flavour, this characteristic is successfully tempered with the sweetness of red and green peppers.

Serves 2

Ingredients

40g/1$^1/_2$ oz butter
1 Spanish onion, coarsely chopped
$^1/_2$ red pepper, deseeded and sliced
$^1/_2$ green pepper, deseeded and sliced
6 lamb's kidneys
100g/3$^1/_2$ oz button mushrooms, sliced
1 medium tomato, peeled and coarsely chopped
salt and ground white pepper

1 Melt the butter in a heavy-based flameproof casserole, or a large sauté pan, set over medium heat. Add the onion and peppers, then stir for 1 minute. Add the kidneys. Stir to combine then sauté for 5 minutes, or until the onion softens, stirring occasionally.

2 Mix in the mushrooms and tomato. Season to taste. Cover with a lid and simmer gently for about 3 minutes or until the mushrooms flop and yield their juices.

3 Remove from the heat. Adjust seasoning and serve hot or tepid, with a rice or bulgur pilav.

Choban Kavurma

The chief hallmark of this casserole of lamb, in which juicy chunks of meat intermingle with tomatoes, peppers and onions, is that it is made without cooking oil or additional fat of any kind. The ingredients are stewed simply in their natural juices in a covered pan. Choose a casserole or sauteuse with a heavy base which conducts heat well, otherwise the ingredients may stick. Middle-neck fillet of lamb is a favourite choice of cut because its surrounding fat helps to provide moisture in the initial stages of cooking. The fat can be discarded at a later stage if you wish. An alternative cut is boneless shoulder. If you use leg meat, you will probably have to add some cooking oil to the pan to compensate for the meat's leanness.

Serves 4

Ingredients

565g/1lb 4oz middle-neck fillet of lamb, cut into small pieces
1 Spanish onion, coarsely chopped
1 small red pepper, deseeded and cut into 1cm/$^1/_2$ inch pieces
1 small green pepper, deseeded and cut into 1cm/$^1/_2$ inch pieces
1 extra-large tomato, or 2 smaller ones, peeled and coarsely chopped
1 teaspoon dried crushed chilli (optional)
salt and ground white pepper
$^1/_2$ teaspoon finely chopped fresh or dried oregano, or dried rosemary

1 Put the lamb in a heavy-based flameproof casserole, or a sauté pan with a lid. Set the pan over a low to medium heat. Cover and leave the meat to sweat for 7–10 minutes or until it has exuded several tablespoons of juice. During this time, remove the lid and stir the meat occasionally to prevent sticking.
2 Adjust the heat to low. Add the onion and red and green peppers. Stir continuously for 2–3 minutes to prevent premature browning. Cover and leave the vegetables to sweat for 4 minutes.
3 Stir in the tomato and, if you wish, the dried chilli. Season to taste. Cover and leave to simmer for a further 3 or 4 minutes or until the tomato has flopped and the onion is cooked. Just before serving, stir in the fresh or dried oregano or dried rosemary. Serve with a rice or bulgur pilav.

Kuzu Kapama

This delightful casserole of spring lamb, spring onions and lettuce tastes particularly ravishing during the spring and summer months when the flavour of the main ingredients is at a peak. In keeping with the sprightly spirit of the dish, the sauce is light and fragrant. The recipe's call for shoulder blades of lamb can be adapted to good-quality boneless stewing lamb, but the latter will require a shorter cooking time. In Turkey, we serve the dish with the meat still clinging to the bone; but you could remove the bones prior to presentation if you wish. New potatoes with fresh mint make a good accompaniment.

Serves 4

Ingredients

about 5 tablespoons olive oil
4 shoulder blades of lamb, each weighing about 455g/1lb, cut across into 225/^{1}/$_2$ lb sections, trimmed of fat
salt and freshly ground black pepper
^{1}/$_2$ Spanish onion, finely chopped
1 red pepper, deseeded and cut into small even pieces
1 green pepper, deseeded and cut into small even pieces
2 teaspoons dried rosemary
1 tablespoon dried marjoram
1 tablespoon tomato purée
about 570ml/1 pint/2^1/$_2$ cups hot vegetable stock or water
3 medium tomatoes, peeled and cut into wedges
12–16 slender spring onions, topped and tailed, and the fatter ones split lengthwise
1 small to medium lettuce, preferably webb's wonder or cos, the leaves separated
2 tablespoons finely chopped fresh marjoram or flat-leaf parsley

1 Heat 2 tablespoons of the oil in a large deep-sided saucepan set over a low heat. Add the pieces of lamb, cover and sweat gently for about 8 minutes, turning once or twice.

2 Add salt and black pepper to taste, the onion, red and green peppers, dried rosemary and dried marjoram. Stir well. Add more oil if the pan appears dry or if ingredients stick. Cover and sweat gently for about 5 minutes or until the onion has softened slightly.

3 Stir in the tomato purée and hot stock or water. Bring the liquid to a light boil, add the tomatoes then cover the casserole and simmer it, either over a very low heat on a heat-resistant mat, or in an oven preheated to 160°C/325°F/gas mark 3 for about 1 hour.

4 Taste and adjust seasoning. Add the spring onions and lay the lettuce leaves on top. Cover again with the lid and continue to simmer for about 8 minutes or until the lettuce leaves have wilted.

5 Scatter with fresh herbs and serve straight away with new potatoes garnished with fresh mint, or with rice or pasta.

Meyhane Pilav

Combined with lamb and robust flavourings, this bulgur-based pilav is a favourite in many Turkish households. It is also served regularly in the meyhane, or men's drinking clubs, where it is valued for its restorative properties and its sense of comfort food.

Serves 6

Ingredients

40g/1 1/2 oz butter
1 tablespoon olive oil
500g/1lb 2oz middle-neck or lean stewing lamb, diced
salt
1/2 large Spanish onion, finely chopped
3 Charleston peppers or 1 medium green pepper, deseeded and finely chopped
5 tablespoons tomato purée
1 vegetable or chicken stock cube, dissolved in one teacup of boiling water
2 pinches paprika
2 1/2 –3 teaspoons dried crushed chillies or chilli powder
3 medium tomatoes, peeled and finely chopped
500g/1lb 2oz bulgur, washed several times and drained
ground white pepper

1 Heat the butter and oil in a deep-sided saucepan and sauté the lamb until it colours; season with salt. Cover the pan and sweat the lamb over very low heat for about 5 minutes. Stir in the onion and Charleston or green pepper, and sweat for a further 10 minutes.

2 Add the tomato purée, stock, paprika, dried chillies and tomatoes, stirring well to achieve a smooth mixture. If necessary, add boiling water to ensure that the ingredients are just covered. Cover, and simmer very gently for one hour. During this time, add water if the sauce becomes too reduced and sticky.

3 Stir in the bulgur and enough boiling water to cover by about 1cm/1/2 inch. Bring to a boil, lower the heat, season, cover, and simmer for 20 minutes or until the liquid is absorbed and the bulgur plump and tender.

4 Before serving the bulgur, place a cloth beneath the lid of the saucepan and put it in a warm place to rest for 10–15 minutes. Fluff it up with a fork before you take it to the table.

Albanian Liver

When diced lamb's liver is jumped around in sizzling oil and heady spices, Turkish style, it becomes an altogether more exciting proposition than its western counterpart. Hot oil ensures that the outside is seized so that juices can be sealed within. At Sofra, the chefs painstakingly remove the thin, but tough, outer membrane from the liver; and this makes a world of difference to the finished result. A rice accompaniment, such as Bademli Pilav *(see page 46)*, is a classic partner for this dish. A garnish of salad, such as the one given below, is also a good idea, although Cacık *(see page 14)* and Hünkar Beğendi *(see page 22)* would be intelligent choices too.

Serves 4

Ingredients

565g/1lb 4oz lamb's liver, washed and dried
salt
$^1/_2$ teaspoon hot or mild chilli powder
about 4 tablespoons flour
6 tablespoons vegetable oil
a good pinch of paprika

For the salad garnish
1 small red onion, finely chopped
1 medium tomato, peeled and finely chopped
2 tablespoons finely chopped fresh parsley
a pinch of dried, crushed chillies

1 To remove the membrane which covers the liver, lift up a small piece of it with the tip of a small sharp knife and gradually peel it away. If you like, put a piece of ice on the liver for 5 minutes to make the peeling easy. Dice the liver into 2.5cm/1 inch pieces. Sprinkle it first with salt, next with chilli powder, then rub the liver to make it absorb the flavourings. Coat evenly with flour, using a plastic bag if you wish.

2 Prepare the salad garnish by mixing together the chopped red onion, tomato, parsley and dried chillies, then chopping everything together; set aside.

3 Heat the oil in a large frying pan. Add the liver. After a few seconds, shake the pan and turn the liver quickly to seize it all round. Sprinkle with paprika. Continue to turn the liver until it has been in the pan for a total of about 2 minutes. Test for doneness: the centre should be juicy and slightly pink.

4 Serve with the salad garnish and a rice accompaniment.

İncik

In this lamb and vegetable casserole, the flavouring of the sauce owes much to the spicy orange taste and aroma of ground coriander mingling with sieved tomatoes. Garnish vegetables of cherry tomatoes, courgettes, white pearl onions and new potatoes are used in the recipe below; but these can be varied to suit seasons and preferences. Fresh peas, okra, broad beans and mangetout are just a few of the possibilities. The shanks, which can come from the knuckle-end of either the hind leg or the fore leg, may have to be ordered in advance from your butcher. Each shank makes a very hearty meal. For daintier portions, you may want to ask the butcher to cut the shanks in half, in which case this recipe would feed eight.

Serves 4

Ingredients

about 5 tablespoons flour
2 teaspoons ground white pepper
4 teaspoons ground coriander
4 lamb shanks, each weighing 340–455g/12oz–1lb
6 tablespoons olive oil
2 small cloves of garlic, finely chopped
$^1/_2$ large Spanish onion, finely chopped
500ml/18fl oz/2$^1/_4$ cups passata
395g/14oz canned chopped tomatoes
1$^1/_2$ tablespoons dried thyme
2 teaspoons caster sugar
a pinch of paprika
peel and juice of 1 orange
salt
395g/14oz courgettes, trimmed, halved lengthwise, sliced diagonally, then parboiled for 4 minutes
225g/$^1/_2$ lb new potatoes, parboiled for 8–10 minutes
170g/6oz white pearl onions, or tiny shallots, peeled and parboiled for about 8 minutes
about 140ml/5fl oz/$^2/_3$ cup vegetable stock or water (optional)
225g/$^1/_2$ lb cherry tomatoes, preferably skinned
3 tablespoons finely chopped fresh coriander
2 tablespoons finely chopped fresh oregano

1 Put the flour, white pepper and 2 teaspoons of the ground coriander into a large plastic bag. Add the lamb shanks and shake the bag to coat the meat.

2 Heat 4 tablespoons of the oil in a large flameproof casserole set over a medium heat. Add the shanks and sauté them, turning several times, for 8 minutes or until evenly browned.

3 Add the remaining oil, the garlic and onion. Reduce the heat, cover, and gently sweat the ingredients for 7 minutes or until the onion has softened. Add the passata, chopped tomatoes, thyme, sugar, paprika, orange peel and juice, salt and remaining ground coriander. Raise the heat and bring to a light boil, scraping the bottom of the pan to dissolve caramelized juices.

4 Check seasoning. Cover the casserole and simmer it, either over a low heat, or in an oven preheated to 180°C/350°F/gas mark 4 for about 1 hour or until the lamb is tender and the sauce slightly reduced.

5 Discard the orange peel. Transfer the ingredients to a clean pan – or wash the one in use. If you like, refrigerate the casserole overnight, then remove any fat from the surface with kitchen towels.

6 About 25 minutes before you are ready to serve the casserole, bring it gently to simmering point. Add the courgettes, potatoes and onions. If more liquid is required to support the vegetables, add a little stock or water. After 8 minutes, add the cherry tomatoes. Taste and adjust seasoning, then cook everything together for a further 5 minutes or so. Just before serving, stir in the fresh herbs.

Grills and Barbecues

Sofra Special Kebab

Variations of the classic Lamb Şiş kebab *(see page 74)* abound. This one incorporates red and green peppers and onions which heighten the natural sweetness of the lamb and lend colour. You can also include garlic and whole chilli peppers. In fact, you can let your personal fancies run riot; but remember not to squash the items too closely together. The marinade can also be varied. The Onion Juice Marinade below, which has been used in Turkish cookery from time immemorial, is great; but if the necessary onion-grating does not suit your eyes, then use the Milk and Oil Marinade *(see page 74)*.

Serves 4

Ingredients

900g/2lb loin fillet, or boneless leg of lamb
about 1½ red or green peppers, deseeded and cut into 20 × 4cm/1¾ inch pieces
2 medium onions, cut into wedges

For the Onion Juice Marinade
1 large Spanish onion
1 teaspoon ground cinnamon
140ml/5fl oz/⅔ cup olive oil
salt and ground white pepper

4 wedges lemon to garnish
1 teaspoon dried oregano (optional)

1 Trim away all fat from the lamb and cut it into 24 even-sized cubes of about 4cm/1¾ inches; set aside.
2 For the marinade, grate the onion using the finest blades of a grater, set over a plate. Combine with the remaining marinade ingredients. Add the lamb. Cover. Marinate for at least several hours.
3 Remove the lamb cubes from the marinade and thread them onto 4 × 30cm/12 inch skewers, starting with a piece of lamb and alternating with pieces of pepper and onion. Sprinkle with dried oregano.
4 Grill the kebabs over charcoal or beneath a preheated, hot oven grill. Cook, turning, and basting occasionally with the marinade, until done to your liking. For medium-pink meat, allow about 5 minutes on each side.
5 Garnish with lemon. If you like, add a touch of dried oregano. Serve with rice and accompaniments.

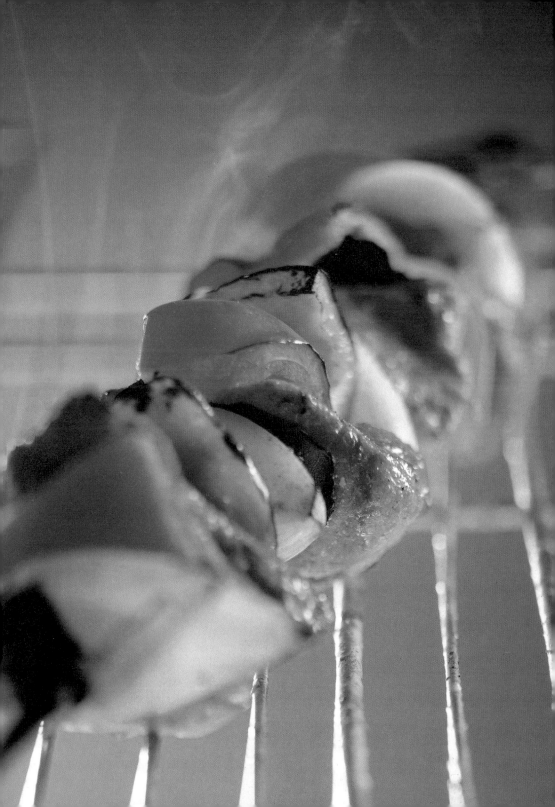

Şiş Köfte

Şiş Köfte differs from Lamb Şiş *(see page 74)* in that the meat is ground to a smooth paste rather than being cut into chunky pieces. Both types of şiş are, of course, skewered and grilled but, again, there is a difference: köfte paste is artfully shaped around the skewer whereas chunky pieces are impaled. The shaping of köfte may sound awesome, but it is not difficult as long as the skewer is wide and flat. At Sofra, our köfte skewers are 1cm/½ inch wide and 45cm/18 inches long. If you cannot obtain these, then forego skewers completely and make the köfte paste into patties, which can be grilled or fried like hamburgers. No matter which form they take, köfte remain a wonderfully light, tasty way of eating lamb. Serve with yogurt, salad, rice or tucked into pitta bread which you have lined with salad leaves and herbs.

Serves 4

Ingredients

950g/2lb 2oz lean minced lamb
½ bunch flat-leaf parsley, stalks discarded, the leaves finely chopped
1 Spanish onion, finely chopped
1 red pepper, deseeded and finely chopped
1 green pepper, deseeded and finely chopped
1 tablespoon paprika
½ teaspoon bicarbonate of soda
salt and ground white pepper
about 3 tablespoons olive oil, for oiling your hands and utensils
4 wedges lemon to garnish

1 Mix together all the ingredients except the olive oil. Using a food processor, process the mixture, in batches if necessary, to a smooth, sticky paste.
2 Working with well-oiled hands, divide the mixture into 8 pieces. Squeeze each piece around a 1cm/½ inch wide skewer, starting at the skewer's pointed end, then pushing the paste along the skewer to distribute it evenly. Alternatively, you can pat the 8 pieces into patties about 7cm/3 inches in diameter.
3 Grill skewered köfte over charcoal or beneath a preheated, hot oven grill. Brush the grill with oil to prevent the meat from sticking. Cook for 6–15 minutes, depending on your preferred degree of doneness, turning frequently. Grill or fry patties for several minutes on each side.
4 Serve with wedges of lemon and the accompaniments of your choice.

Lamb Şiş

This is seasoned, skewered lamb at its best: the caress of spice so light as to awaken the meat's flavour without overwhelming it; the texture of the meat so tender that it can be cut with a spoon. The Milk and Oil Marinade *(below)* which is used for this Lamb Şiş is a favourite at Sofra. The milk element makes the lamb as tender as the luxurious milk-fed variety. Because this is a purist Lamb Şiş, with nothing but meat on the skewer, you can go to town with elaborate salads and accompaniments if you wish. Options include Bademli Pilav *(see page 46)*, Cacık *(see page 14)* and Hünkar Beğendi *(see page 22)*.

Serves 4

Ingredients

900g/2lb loin fillet, or boneless leg of lamb

For the Milk and Oil Marinade
200ml/7fl oz/³/₄ cup milk
200ml/7fl oz/³/₄ cup vegetable oil
2–3 teaspoons paprika
¹/₂ teaspoon cumin
about ¹/₂ teaspoon salt
¹/₂ teaspoon ground white pepper

4 wedges lemon to garnish

1 Trim away all fat from the lamb and cut it into 24 even-sized cubes of about 4cm/1³/₄ inches; set aside.
2 In a large dish, or in a plastic container with a lid, combine the marinade ingredients and stir well. Add the cubes of lamb, turning them in the marinade. Cover and leave in a cool place, or in the refrigerator, for several hours, preferably overnight.
3 Remove the cubes of lamb from the marinade and thread them onto 4 × 30cm/12 inch skewers.

4 Grill the kebabs over charcoal or beneath a preheated, hot oven grill, close to the heat source. Cook the kebabs, turning them occasionally and basting with the marinade, until done to your liking. For medium-pink meat, allow about 5 minutes on each side.
5 Serve one skewer to each guest, removing the skewer at table. Offer lemon and chosen accompaniments.

Chicken Şiş

In Turkey, chicken is almost as popular as it is in the west. Its breast meat is easy to dice and skewer as in this şiş dish; and its unassertive flavour lends itself to a variety of different marinades and sauces. At Sofra, we frequently use the Milk and Oil Marinade *(see page 74)* for chicken as well as for lamb. The main thing is to choose a marinade which will suit your personal choice of flavourings as well as the meal as a whole. Whenever I plan to serve Chicken Şiş with Spicy Tomato and Sweet Pepper Sauce *(see page 59)*, I invariably choose the Spicy Tomato Marinade *(below)* so that flavours pull together and create an impact.

Serves 4

Ingredients

For the Spicy Tomato Marinade
2 cloves of garlic, crushed to a pulp
$1/2$ teaspoon paprika
2 tablespoons lemon juice
2 teaspoons tomato purée
salt and ground white pepper
140ml/5fl oz natural yogurt

4 boneless chicken breasts, skinned; each one sliced crosswise into 5 or 6 longish strips

1 In a large bowl, or a plastic container with a lid, mix together the ingredients for the marinade. Immerse the pieces of chicken, cover, and leave to marinate in a cool place or in the refrigerator for at least 5 hours, preferably overnight, turning the chicken occasionally.

2 Remove the pieces of chicken and thread 5 or 6 pieces onto each skewer, pushing the skewer right through the longest part of each piece.

3 Grill the şiş either over charcoal or beneath a preheated, hot oven grill. Cook for about 5 minutes on each side, basting with the marinade when you turn them over.

4 Serve 1 skewer to each guest, removing the skewer at table. Serve with rice and salad and, if you like, the Spicy Tomato and Sweet Pepper Sauce *(see page 59)*.

Chicken Wings in a Lively Marinade

Humble though they may be, chicken wings carry the reassurance that good food does not have to cost a fortune. Wing-meat has a wonderfully full flavour and great succulence. At first sight, though, they do not look very fetching: their awkward scraggy shape is covered with flapping folds of coarse, hairy skin. However, once the scrappy bits are ruthlessly cut away, and the wings halved to make neat compact shapes, their appearance and edibility changes dramatically. Here, a very lively marinade completes the makeover and, once grilled, the wings emerge ready for any table. They are particularly welcome at parties where finger food is in demand.

Serves 4

Ingredients

For the Onion, Chilli and Paprika Marinade
1 Spanish onion
4 small cloves of garlic, crushed to a pulp
1 tablespoon dried, crushed chillies
1½ tablespoons paprika
200ml/7fl oz/¾ cup vegetable oil
salt and ground white pepper

16 chicken wings

1 For the marinade, grate the onion using the finest surface of a grater, set over a plate. Apply pressure so that onion juice flows alongside a slushy pulp. Alternatively, coarsely chop the onion and blend it in a food processor. Discard any stringy bits of onion. Combine the onion juice, pulp, and remaining marinade ingredients. Cover and set aside.

2 Prepare the chicken wings by cutting off and discarding the pointed wing-tips. Trim the sides free of over-hanging skin, hairs and fat, exposing the flesh beneath. Snap the main bone joint to break it, then cut through it to obtain neat pieces of a more or less equal size.

3 Immerse the 32 wing pieces in the marinade, turning to coat them evenly. Cover and leave in a cool place or in the refrigerator, to marinate for at least 5 hours, preferably overnight; turn the pieces occasionally.

4 Remove the chicken wings. Place them on a grill rack with the marinade that clings to them. Grill them either over charcoal or beneath a preheated, hot oven grill about 2.5cm/1 inch away from the heat source. Cook the wings for about 6–7 minutes on each side, or until a golden crust forms and they are done. Baste with the marinade when you turn them over.

5 Serve the wings with rice and salad, or on their own as party finger food.

Roast Chicken with Oregano

In Turkey, the herb that is most widely used for the roasting of a chicken is oregano, although thyme, marjoram, flat-leaf parsley and coriander all find favour from time to time. Anointing the bird with olive oil or softened butter, prior to roasting, is important to prevent drying out and to ensure a good colour and flavour. To guard against the breast being done before the legs have cooked, I start the bird on its side. Remember to turn the bird periodically so that it becomes golden and crisp all round.

Serves 4–6

Ingredients

2¹/₂ teaspoons dried oregano
30g/1oz butter
1 × 1.6kg/3¹/₂ lb chicken
salt and freshly ground black pepper
a few sprigs of fresh oregano (optional)
juice of ¹/₂ lemon
2 tablespoons olive oil
225ml/8fl oz/1 cup chicken stock or wine or water
a few sprigs of fresh oregano or flat-leaf parsley to garnish (optional)

1 Work a good pinch of the dried oregano into the butter. Put this inside the bird along with some salt and pepper, and a few sprigs of fresh oregano if you have them. Sprinkle the outside of the bird with salt, then rub in the lemon juice, the olive oil and the remaining dried oregano. Set the chicken on its side in a snugly fitting roasting tin.

2 Put the chicken in an oven preheated to 200°C/400°F/gas mark 6 and roast it, basting frequently, for about 70 minutes or until done. After 20 minutes of the cooking time, turn the bird on its other side and, after a further 20 minutes, place it breast-up. If the bird's breast colours too quickly, shield it with foil. Test for doneness after 1 hour by pushing a skewer into the thickest part of the bird's thighs. If the juices that flow are clear, the bird is done. If they are pink, roast it for a further 10 minutes then test again.

3 Transfer the bird to a carving platter and wrap it loosely in foil. Leave it to rest briefly. Meanwhile, drain excess fat from the roasting tin, set it over high heat, and add the stock or other liquid. Boil the liquid briskly for several minutes while you stir to scrape up the crusty deposits and dissolve them into a sauce. Strain into a sauceboat.

4 Carve the chicken and serve it garnished with fresh herbs. Offer the sauce and the accompaniments of your choice.

Main Course Fish

Deep-Fried Mussels

This dish of mussels, deep-fried in a crisp, light batter and served with a Tarator Sauce of walnuts, garlic and olive oil, is found virtually all over Turkey. Its popularity excels, though, in Istanbul and in Izmir, where the mussels which come off the Aegean coast are so sumptuous. Most fishmongers will sell the mussels on the shell. When you get them home, scrub them well and remove beards. Discard any that are open or have broken shells. Put them in a pan with a little water and heat them until the shells start to open. Prize the shells fully open with a knife, remove the mussels then wash and drain them on kitchen towels. The sauce, traditionally made with walnuts, is also excellent made with a mixture of hazelnuts and pine kernels.

Serves 4

Ingredients

For the batter
115g/4oz/¹/₂ cup flour
salt
2 eggs, yolks separated from whites
3 tablespoons olive oil
200ml/7fl oz/³/₄ cup pale ale or lager

For the Tarator Sauce
2 slices stale white or brown bread
4 tablespoons wine vinegar or rice vinegar
7 tablespoons walnut or olive oil
115g/4oz/1 cup walnut pieces, coarsely chopped
3 large cloves of garlic, coarsely chopped

40 large mussels, shelled
a small amount of flour
sunflower oil for deep-frying
4 wedges lemon to garnish

1 For the batter, mix together the flour, salt, egg yolks and oil in a bowl. Gradually add the beer and whisk for only as long as it takes to produce a smooth batter. Do not overwork the mixture. Cover the bowl with a towel and leave the batter to rest for at least 1 hour at room temperature – otherwise it will shrink away from the mussels. Just before using the batter, beat the egg whites to soft peaks and fold them into the mixture.

2 While the batter rests, make the sauce: soak the bread in water for several minutes then squeeze out excess moisture. Drop it, in bits, into the bowl of a blender or food processor. Add the vinegar, oil, nuts and garlic and blend to a smooth, thickish sauce. Turn out into a bowl and stir in a little salt to taste.

3 Dust the mussels very lightly in flour. Heat some oil in a deep pan to 190°C/375°F. Dip the mussels into the batter, lightened with egg white, and deep fry them, about 10 at a time, for 3–4 minutes or until golden. Remove and drain on kitchen paper. When all the mussels are done, salt them lightly and serve with wedges of lemon and the Tarator Sauce.

Uskumru Dolması

In Turkey, and especially in Istanbul, mackerel is frequently filleted through its neck openings, its loose flesh removed and mixed with other ingredients, then re-stuffed back through the neck. This method of filleting is worth learning *(see 'Filleting Mackerel', page 83)* because it permits delicious stuffings to be enjoyed free of bones. If you haven't the time to do it, then gut the fish through the belly in the more usual way and leave the bones and flesh intact. The stuffings can be varied. The one below is typically Turkish in its inclusion of walnuts, pine kernels, currants and sweet spice. The garnish of dill and lemon cuts through the oily tendency of the mackerel like a sparkling diamond.

Serves 4

Ingredients

For the stuffing
1 medium Spanish onion, finely chopped
30g/1oz unsalted butter
about 3 tablespoons olive oil
2$\frac{1}{2}$ tablespoons currants, soaked
1$\frac{1}{2}$ tablespoons walnut pieces, finely chopped
1$\frac{1}{2}$ tablespoons pine kernels
$\frac{1}{4}$ teaspoon ground cinnamon
$\frac{1}{4}$ teaspoon allspice
about 2 tablespoons fresh white breadcrumbs
salt and ground white pepper
2 tablespoons finely chopped fresh dill
a little lightly beaten egg

For frying
6–7 tablespoons day-old fine white breadcrumbs
2 tablespoons finely chopped flat-leaf parsley
2 tablespoons finely chopped fresh dill
finely grated zest of 1 lemon
salt and ground white pepper
2 large egg yolks
4 mackerel, gutted (preferably gutted through the gills and filleted, *see page 83*)
4–5 tablespoons olive oil
2 teaspoons finely chopped fresh dill to garnish
4 wedges lemon to garnish

1 To make the stuffing, sweat the onion gently in the butter and oil in a frying pan for about 10 minutes or until soft. Stir in the currants, walnuts, pine kernels, cinnamon, allspice and all the loose, chopped mackerel flesh you may have from filleting through the neck openings. Cook for a further 2 minutes. Transfer to a bowl. Stir in the fresh breadcrumbs, seasoning and dill. Leave to cool. When the stuffing is quite cold, add just enough beaten egg to bind it.

2 While the stuffing cools, prepare the breadcrumb mixture for frying: mix the day-old breadcrumbs, parsley, dill and lemon zest on a large plate and season well. Beat the egg yolks in a wide, shallow bowl.

3 Fill the mackerel with the cold stuffing, using either the neck openings of the fish or its belly.

4 Dip the mackerel in the yolks, then in the breadcrumb mixture. Fry the mackerel for about 5 minutes on each side in hot olive oil. Serve hot or cold, garnished with dill and wedges of lemon.

Filleting Mackerel

Several of the mackerel specialities of Istanbul involve gutting and filleting mackerel without opening the belly. When you buy the mackerel, choose specimens that are absolutely fresh (and have preferably not been frozen), and weigh at least 225g/$\frac{1}{2}$ lb. Make sure that the fishmonger leaves the heads on and the bellies intact. If he wants to gut them through the gills for you, then fine, let him do it. If he hasn't time, then the job is yours – but don't worry because it is very easy.

At home, you will first need to trim away fins and, if the fishmonger has not done it already, gut the mackerel through the gills. To do this, take a mackerel, insert your fingers into the neck openings on both sides of the head, open them out a little, then poke behind the gills and grasp the dark sac that stretches down towards the belly. Pull it out. Often the gills will come away with the sac. If they do not, pull them out and discard them anyway. Wash the fish well and dry it.

The next step is to fillet the fish. Locate a spot along the backbone 5mm/$\frac{1}{4}$ inch from the end of the tail. Move the bone to the right and left to break it. It is helpful if you hear it snap, otherwise feel carefully to make sure it is broken. Break the backbone, in the same way, just below the head. Next, roll the fish to and fro a couple of times on a board, the object of which is to loosen the flesh a little on the inside so that it starts to separate slightly from the bones. Then, with one hand, hold the fish between its head and belly; with the other, insert your fingers into the neck opening, grasp the backbone, wriggle it a bit, then pull it out. Some flesh will come out with the bone. To remove the remaining flesh without tearing the skin, squeeze the fish gently, working from the tail end towards the head, and extract it through the neck opening.

Pick over the extracted flesh carefully and discard any small bones. Chop the flesh evenly and use it according to the instructions of the recipe.

Sardines in Vine Leaves

Sardines, fresh out of the Sea of Marmara, are one of Istanbul's favourite fish. Sizzled over charcoal or jumped about in a tava pan, their distinctly savoury flesh makes an appetizing meze as well as a main course. Sometimes, as here, they are cooked in vine leaves, the lemony edge of which counters the fish's natural oiliness. Often, though, they are simply tossed in flour, fried in hot oil and served with salt and lemon juice. But what about the bones? True devotees claim not even to notice them. But there is a simple way of filleting sardines. It is to slit them along the belly, open them out like a book, lay them skin-side up, then just tap along the back bone with the bottom of a milk bottle or a coffee mug, or similar. You will almost feel the bones parting from the flesh. Turn the fish over, and pull away the bone structure in one piece. Easy. There is also a rather fancy way whereby the belly is left intact and the bones are extracted through the neck openings. It is the same method as for mackerel, which is explained on page 83.

Serves 4

Ingredients

about 20 preserved vine leaves, drained of their brine
about 7 tablespoons olive oil
about 20 fresh sardines, gutted and, preferably, filleted
salt and freshly ground black pepper
4 wedges lemon to garnish
4 large sprigs flat-leaf parsley to garnish

1 Soak the preserved vine leaves for 15 minutes in several changes of cold water; drain and pat dry.
2 Arrange the leaves vein-side up and with the stalk-end, or base, nearest to you. Nip off the stalks and brush with a little of the oil. One by one, position a sardine on a leaf with its tail extending slightly beyond the stalk-end. Add seasoning, then wrap up the sardine in the leaf, exposing a tail and a head at each end. Brush the parcel with a little more of the oil. Repeat until all the sardines are wrapped.

3 Heat the remaining oil in a frying pan. Slide in the sardines, seam-side down, a few at a time, and cook for 4 minutes on each side, or until the fish are done and the leaves have turned a yellowish green. Alternatively, grill them for about 4 minutes on each side.
4 Garnish the sardines with lemon and parsley. Serve with a salad and crusty bread. To eat them, open the vine leaves and sprinkle with lemon juice.

Shrimp Casserole

Serve this aromatic casserole with a pilav and allow the rice to mop up the rich tomato sauce. The foundational sauce (steps 1 and 2), can be prepared well in advance.

Serves 6

Ingredients

30g/1oz butter
3–4 tablespoons olive oil
2 Spanish onions, finely chopped
3 large cloves of garlic, finely chopped
1.6kg/3½ lb ripe tomatoes, peeled and coarsely chopped
3 large sprigs fresh thyme
3 bay leaves
2 teaspoons dried oregano
1 teaspoon allspice berries, crushed
140ml/5fl oz/²/₃ cup red wine or fish stock
salt and ground white pepper
1–2 teaspoons caster sugar
about ¼ teaspoon chilli powder
2 small green peppers, deseeded and finely chopped
EITHER
455g/1 lb cooked brown shrimp in their shells, topped and tailed
OR
1 kg/2¼ lb cooked pink prawns in their shells, peeled
2½ tablespoons finely chopped fresh flat-leaf parsley
6 cooked king prawns to garnish
6 wedges of lemon to garnish

1 In a large, heavy-based saucepan, gently heat the butter and oil and sweat the onions until soft but not coloured. Stir in the garlic and, after a few minutes, add the tomatoes, herbs, allspice and wine or stock. Bring to a light boil, stirring, then adjust the heat to maintain a brisk simmer. Cook uncovered for 30–40 minutes, adding only the tiniest pinch of salt towards the end.

2 Press the tomato sauce through a nylon sieve and discard the solids. Put the sauce in a clean pan and reduce it until it coats a spoon like thick cream. Add seasoning, sugar and chilli powder to taste.

3 Just before you are ready to serve, add the green peppers and prawns to the sauce. Simmer over a low heat for about 5 minutes, taking care not to overcook the prawns. Stir in the parsley. Serve, with a pilav, and garnish with prawns and lemon.

Salmon in a Foil Parcel

In Turkey, the method of cooking fish in a paper parcel is an ancient one. In bygone days, the choice was parchment paper; nowadays it is chiefly foil. The aim is the same though: to create a moist atmosphere in which the fish can steam to succulent perfection. With the following recipe, extra moisture is supplied by the natural juices of the surrounding vegetables – sweet red and green peppers and mangetout. Small new potatoes are also included so that the parcel is a complete dish and a good choice for relaxed entertaining.

Serves 1

Ingredients

$^1/_2$ Spanish onion, finely chopped
2 tablespoons olive oil
55g/2oz butter, diced
$^1/_2$ red pepper, deseeded and thinly sliced
$^1/_2$ green pepper, deseeded and thinly sliced
7 mangetout
2 small new potatoes, parboiled for 6 minutes
$^1/_2$ teaspoon crushed black peppercorns
3 dried bay leaves
1 teaspoon light soy sauce
1 tablespoon lemon juice
2 slices lemon
170g/6oz salmon steak or fillet of salmon
$^1/_2$ medium tomato, peeled and finely chopped (optional)
salt and ground white pepper

1 In a large sauté pan, gently sauté the onion in the oil and half the butter for 3 minutes. Add the peppers, mangetout, potatoes, peppercorns, bay leaves, soy sauce and the juice and slices of lemon. Sauté until the vegetables are a little more than half-cooked, stirring to prevent browning. Remove from the heat.

2 Lay the salmon on a piece of double-thickness foil, large enough to enclose the ingredients loosely. Add the remaining butter and the vegetables. If there is less than 2 tablespoons of juice, include a little water or half a chopped tomato. Season, and seal the parcel.

3 Put the parcel on a baking sheet in an oven preheated to 230°C/450°F/gas mark 8. Immediately lower the heat to 190°C/375°F/gas mark 5. Cooking time will vary: for a shallow fillet, allow about 12 minutes. For a 2.5cm/1 inch thick steak, allow about 20 minutes.

4 To serve the salmon, open the parcel at table and, if you wish, remove the salmon skin. Use a spatula to transfer the entire parcel to an individual serving plate.

Spiced Cod Steamed Beneath Spinach

Fresh, light and colourful, this dish is a marvellous showcase for healthy eating. It is easy to make in the bargain and, because you can prepare most of it in advance (steps 1–3), good for entertaining. The fish is seized in oil and spice to start, then finished by steaming beneath layers of spinach. Tomatoes assist in creating a moist atmosphere. There are two shopping tips to pass on: the first is to avoid baby spinach – larger leaves are preferable here; the second is to buy cod fillet that is thick-cut and skinless (see 'Buying Cod', page 93).

Serves 4

Ingredients

680–800g/1lb 8oz–1lb 12oz prime, 2.5cm/1 inch thick cod fillet, skinned and cut into 4 × 10cm/4 inch squares
salt
1 heaped tablespoon flour
1$^1/_4$ teaspoons turmeric
7 tablespoons olive oil
55g/2oz/$^1/_2$ cup onion, finely chopped
1 medium clove of garlic, finely chopped
30g/1oz fresh ginger root, peeled and coarsely chopped
1$^1/_2$ teaspoons cumin
2 teaspoons ground coriander
455g/1lb tomatoes, peeled and coarsely chopped
freshly ground black pepper
5 tablespoons passata
$^1/_2$ teaspoon caster sugar
200g/7oz fresh spinach, washed and with tough stems removed

1 Season the cod with salt and coat it lightly with flour and $^1/_4$ teaspoon of the turmeric. Heat 5 tablespoons of the oil in a deep saucepan set over low heat. Cook the fish, in batches if necessary, for 30 seconds on each side; remove and set aside.

2 Add the remaining oil to the pan. Gently sauté the onion, garlic and two-thirds of the ginger for 7 minutes or until the onion is soft but not coloured. Stir in the remaining turmeric, the cumin, coriander, tomatoes and seasoning to taste. Cover, and simmer for 3 minutes.

3 Off the heat, return the fish to the pan, spooning over the tomato mixture. Mix the passata with salt, pepper and sugar, then spoon it over the fish. Add the remaining ginger. Arrange the spinach on top leaving no gaps at the edge. Cover the pan with a lid.

4 When you are almost ready to serve the dish, return the pan to a low to medium heat. Cook for about 6 minutes or until the fish has cooked through and the spinach has flopped.

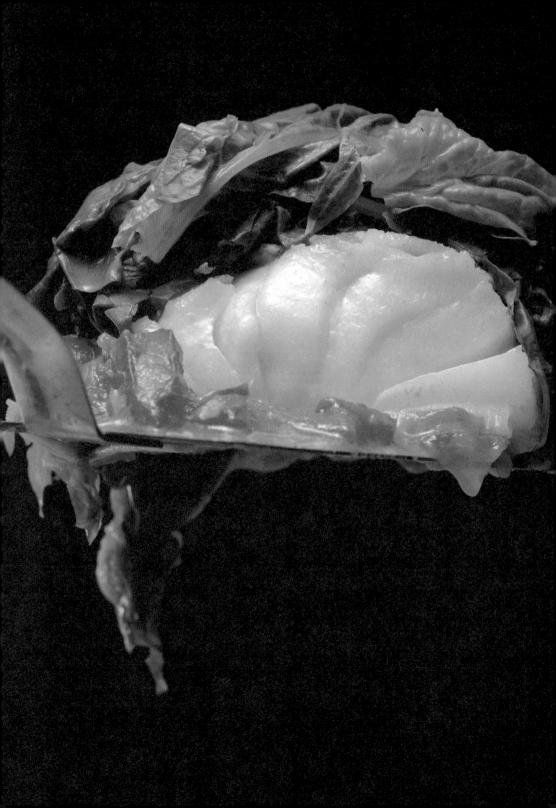

Halibut in a Creamy Pasta Sauce

Halibut needs a good sauce and this one is sublime: the smoothness of the sauce, gained from its base of cream and ribbon pasta, finds lively contrast in the interesting textures and flavours of its supporting vegetables, herbs and spices. Although my preference, on this occasion, is to use ground ginger for its softness, you can use chopped fresh ginger if you prefer.

Serves 1

Ingredients

$1/_2$ Spanish onion, thinly sliced
$1/_2$ red pepper, deseeded and thinly sliced
$1/_2$ green pepper, deseeded and thinly sliced
2 dried bay leaves
1 vegetable stock cube, finely crumbled
2 tablespoons olive oil
freshly ground black pepper
225g/8oz halibut steak
salt
about 1 tablespoon clarified butter, or olive oil for brushing the halibut
225g/8oz fresh ribbon pasta such as tagliatelle, parboiled and drained
1–2 pinches turmeric
2 pinches ground ginger
2 tablespoons double cream
1 tablespoon finely chopped fresh dill or a mixture of chervil and chives

1 Sauté the onion, peppers, bay leaves and stock cube in the oil for 7 minutes or until the onion softens, stirring continuously. Add pepper. Set aside, covered.
2 Season the halibut with salt. Brush it with a little butter or oil and place beneath a low to medium grill for 5–8 minutes on each side or until almost done. Remove its skin and bone. Lay the fish on a piece of double-thickness foil large enough to enclose the ingredients loosely. Top with the pasta. Stir the turmeric, ginger and cream into the reserved vegetable mixture. Taste, and adjust seasoning. Spoon this sauce over the pasta. Scatter over the fresh herbs. Seal the parcel.
3 Put the parcel on a baking sheet in an oven preheated to 190°C/375°F/gas mark 5 for 5–10 minutes or until the halibut is done and the ingredients are heated through.
4 To serve the fish, open the parcel at table and use a spatula to transfer the entire parcel to an individual serving plate.

Brochette of Swordfish

This Turkish speciality of grilled skewered swordfish can be adapted to suit other types of firm-fleshed fish, such as monkfish or halibut. Slices of tomato and lemon are the classic skewer partners; but I find such slices too unstable for the skewer and prefer to use cherry tomatoes. If you are resigned to slices, cut them fairly thick. I also add bay leaves and pieces of sweet pepper or Charleston pepper. For a hotter taste, you could use chilli peppers instead.

Serves 4

Ingredients

For the marinade
2 small cloves of garlic
salt
about $1/2$ teaspoon paprika
2 tablespoons lemon juice
3 tablespoons olive oil
ground white pepper
1 small onion, thinly sliced
4 bay leaves, crumbled

680g/1$1/2$ lb filleted swordfish or other firm white fish, cut into 4cm/1$1/2$ inch pieces
about 20 bay leaves
about 20 cherry tomatoes
2 small red peppers or 4 Charleston peppers, deseeded and cut into 3cm/1$1/4$ inch pieces

For the dressing
2 tablespoons lemon juice
3 tablespoons olive oil
1 tablespoon finely chopped fresh dill or flat-leaf parsley

4 wedges lemon to garnish

1 To make the marinade, crush the garlic to a smooth paste, preferably using a pestle and mortar and a little salt. Add the paprika, lemon juice, oil and sufficient salt and pepper to season the fish. Pour this over the diced fish. Scatter the slices of onion and crumbled bay leaves on top and around the fish. Cover and leave in a cool place or in the refrigerator for 1–2 hours.

2 Remove the pieces of fish and thread them onto 4 skewers, starting and finishing with bay leaves and alternating the fish with cherry tomatoes, bay leaves and pieces of pepper. Baste with a little of the marinade.

3 Arrange the skewers either over a charcoal fire or beneath a medium to hot oven grill. Grill, basting with the marinade and turning frequently, for about 10 minutes or until the fish is tender. Meanwhile, stir together the ingredients for the dressing.

4 Serve straight away, accompanied by the dressing and a rice or bulgur pilav. A garnish of lemon wedges may also be added.

Steamed Cod in a Pink Tomato Sauce

The sauce here is made from concentrated tomatoes smoothed with cream and a little white wine. The cod steams in the vapours from this sauce, along with aromatic vegetables. Steaming takes place initially in a covered pan on the hob and, finally, in a foil parcel in the oven. This process is a boon because you can prepare the pan-stage in advance (steps 1–2) and complete the final stages, which take just 5 minutes or so, at your leisure.

Serves 1

Ingredients

30g/1oz butter
1 Spanish onion, thinly sliced
2 dried bay leaves
2 small new potatoes, parboiled for 6 minutes
$^1/_4$ lemon, peel discarded
$^1/_2$ medium tomato, peeled and coarsely chopped
1 fish stock cube, finely crumbled
salt and freshly ground black pepper
285ml/10fl oz/1$^1/_3$ cups passata
200ml/7fl oz/$^3/_4$ cup double cream
2 tablespoons dry white wine
225g/$^1/_2$ lb cod fillet, skinned
1 tablespoon chopped fresh basil or flat-leaf parsley

1 In a large sauté pan, melt the butter over a low heat. Add the onion, bay leaves, potatoes, lemon, tomato, stock cube and seasoning. Sauté the ingredients uncovered for about 8 minutes or until the onion has softened.
2 Add the passata, then the cream, then the wine, stirring after each addition. Cover and simmer for 3 minutes. Slide in the cod fillet and coat it with the sauce. Cover, and simmer gently for 8–10 minutes or until the cod is almost done, turning it over after 4 minutes. Lay the cod on a piece of double-thickness foil, large enough to enclose the ingredients loosely. Spoon over the vegetables and cream sauce. Adjust seasoning and add the basil or parsley. Seal the parcel.
3 Put the parcel on a baking sheet in an oven preheated to 190°C/375°F/gas mark 5 for 5 minutes or until the fish is done and all the ingredients are heated through.
4 To serve the fish, open the parcel at table and use a spatula to transfer the entire parcel to an individual serving plate.

Buying Cod

For the recipe for Spiced Cod Steamed Beneath Spinach *(see page 88)*, and for other similar recipes requiring that cod fillet be steamed, it is important that the fish does not become over-cooked before the other ingredients are properly done and their flavours intermingled.

To achieve this, the cod fillet must be of the thick variety, about 2.5cm/1 inch at its thickest part, rather than the thin, flat kind which resembles a credit card and cooks too quickly. Ideally, the fillet should also be skinned.

Fresh fish counters, at most large supermarkets as well as at the fishmongers, usually sell two types of cod fillet nowadays: the so-called 'standard' fillet, which is thin and grey-skinned; and the 'prime' fillet, which is very chunky, skinned – and just what you need.

Red Mullet in Boats of Yellow Pepper

Dill and star anise are used here to give hints of anise flavouring to delicate red mullet, which is known in Turkey as both barbunya and tekir. Because the blushing crimson skin of red mullet is easily damaged if the fish are fried or grilled, I cook these fish, with their flavourings, in foil in the oven. Their presentation is in boat-shaped yellow peppers which have been separately grilled and skinned. Red or green peppers may, of course, be substituted for yellow. It is not usual practice to gut mullet that are small. I usually gut them, either through the gut or the gills, if they weigh more than 200g/7oz. Ideally, ask the fishmonger to do this for you, as well as the all-important scaling.

Serves 2

Ingredients

2 × 255g/9oz red mullet, scaled, trimmed of tough fins and gutted if required
about 5 dried star anise
zest and juice of 1 lemon
salt
3 tablespoons olive oil
1 clove of garlic, finely chopped
2 extra-large tomatoes, peeled and finely chopped
$1/_2$ teaspoon caster sugar
freshly ground black pepper
4 large sprigs fresh dill
2 large yellow (or red or green) peppers
2 teaspoons finely chopped fresh dill
4 sprigs fresh mint to garnish
4 small wedges lemon to garnish

1 With a sharp knife, score each mullet in a criss-cross pattern on both sides. Pick out about 10 seeds from the star anise. Crush the seeds, either with a pestle and mortar or with a rolling pin. Mix the ground seeds with the lemon zest and juice and salt. Work this mixture into the scored fish, then brush it with 1 tablespoon of the oil; set aside to marinate briefly.

2 Meanwhile, sauté the garlic in the remaining oil until soft. Add the tomatoes and cook for about 5 minutes or until they reduce to a rough-textured sauce. Add sugar, salt and pepper to taste; allow to cool slightly.

3 Centre the sauce on a sheet of double-thickness foil, large enough to envelop the fish. Place the fish on top and add the sprigs of dill. Seal the parcel.

4 Transfer the parcel to a baking sheet in an oven preheated to 180°C/350°F/gas mark 4. Cook the fish for 20 minutes or until done.

5 Meanwhile, cut the peppers in half lengthwise and remove the seeds, membrane and stalk. Put the peppers curved-side up beneath a hot grill for about 10 minutes or until the skin blisters thoroughly. Rinse under cold water and peel away the skin.

6 Put the 2 halves of each pepper on to serving plates with their wide ends butting together, so that they resemble boats. Unwrap the fish. Discard the sprigs of dill and, if you like, remove the heads from the fish. Spoon the tomato sauce around the pepper boats and arrange the fish inside. Sprinkle the chopped dill over the fish and garnish the sauce with the mint and wedges of lemon.

Monkfish with Sweet Spices

The Turkish tendency of putting sweet spices, especially cinnamon, with basically savoury ingredients is exploited to the full here with monkfish, whose flesh leans towards sweetness so readily. The monkfish tails sit on a bed of spinach which, because of its natural sweetness, is the perfect accompaniment. A garnish of prawns complements the luscious flavours all round.

Serves 4

Ingredients

$^1/_4$ teaspoon ground cinnamon
$^1/_4$ teaspoon ground ginger
several pinches of ground cloves
several pinches of ground nutmeg
1kg/2lb 4oz spinach, washed, tough stems removed
salt
4 monkfish tails on the bone, each weighing 395–455g/14–16oz, trimmed of tail tips and fins
about 2 tablespoons olive oil
ground white pepper
4 large sprigs fresh coriander or flat-leaf parsley
125ml/4fl oz/$^1/_2$ cup fish stock or white wine
40g/1$^1/_2$ oz unsalted butter, diced
170g/6oz prawns in their shells, peeled
4 tablespoons double cream
4 whole prawns to garnish
4 slices lemon to garnish

1 Mix together the cinnamon, the ginger, the cloves and the nutmeg; set aside.
2 Cook the spinach in salted boiling water for about 2 minutes. Drain the spinach, refresh it under cold water, drain again, squeeze out excess moisture, then chop it and set aside under clingfilm.
3 Make a 7.5cm/3 inch slit along the backbone of each monkfish tail, leaving the flesh intact at each end so that you have a pocket. Rub the fish with the oil, some seasoning and the spice mixture. Put a sprig of coriander or parsley in each pocket, and transfer the tails to a heavy roasting dish. Drizzle over the fish stock or wine. Cover the fish with greaseproof paper, spread with about one-third of the butter.
4 Bake the monkfish in an oven preheated to 220°C/425°F/gas mark 7 for 5 minutes, then reduce the heat to 190°C/375°F/gas mark 5, and cook for a further 30 minutes or until lightly done.
5 Strain the cooking juices of the monkfish into a saucepan. Cover the monkfish again and keep it warm while you heat through the peeled prawns in the cooking juices. In a separate pan, heat through the spinach in half the remaining butter and the cream; season it well. Spread out the spinach on a large warmed serving dish. Arrange the monkfish on top. Discard the herbs from the pockets and replace with the garnish of whole prawns and slices of lemon.
6 Remove the prawns from the heat and stir in the last of the butter. When it melts, pour a little of this sauce over the monkfish, and serve the rest separately. Serve the dish straight away.

Swordfish with Peppers, Tomatoes and Olives

For this straightforward rustic dish, swordfish steaks are baked in the oven beneath a layer of sweet peppers and tomatoes. The vegetables help to protect the fish from drying out as it cooks, while their juices, mingled with herbs and spice, become an integral part of the sauce. A mixture of fresh and canned tomatoes is used to produce a pleasing balance of texture, juice and colour. The recipe also suits cod steaks and firm-fleshed white fish as a whole.

Serves 4

Ingredients

2–3 tablespoons olive oil
salt and freshly ground black pepper
4 × 225g/¹/₂ lb swordfish or cod steaks
¹/₂ medium onion, very thinly sliced
2 cloves of garlic, crushed or finely chopped
1 small green pepper, deseeded and sliced
¹/₂ medium red pepper, deseeded and sliced
¹/₂ teaspoon dried oregano
¹/₂ teaspoon ground coriander
¹/₂ teaspoon dried crushed chillies
a pinch of paprika
2 medium tomatoes, peeled and finely chopped
400g/14oz canned tomatoes
¹/₂ teaspoon caster sugar
55g/2oz black pitted olives
grated zest of 1 lemon to garnish
2¹/₂ tablespoons finely chopped fresh flat-leaf parsley to garnish

1 Brush a shallow ovenproof dish with a little of the oil. Season the fish well and arrange it in a single layer in the dish. Drizzle over most of the remaining oil. Add a layer of onion, garlic, green pepper and red pepper. Sprinkle over the dried herbs, coriander, chillies and paprika.

2 Add the chopped fresh tomatoes. Drizzle over the last few drops of oil. Set aside.

3 Press the canned tomatoes through a nylon sieve set over a bowl. Season the purée with salt, pepper and sugar. Spoon over the fish and cover with foil.

4 Bake in an oven preheated to 190°C/375°F/gas mark 5 for 40 minutes.

5 Remove the foil, add the olives and return the dish to the oven for a further 5 minutes. Mix the zest of lemon with the parsley and garnish the fish with this mixture. Serve immediately.

Pasta and Pide

Pasta with Green Lentils

Pasta works with subtlety here, supporting a dominant grouping of green lentils, red and green peppers, tomatoes and aromatic vegetables. Chilli and fresh dill keep flavours alert and clean-tasting. To get the best results – in terms of both flavour and appearance – chop the vegetables finely and use pasta that is dainty in shape. Small is beautiful with this dish. Regards the lentils, check packet instructions to see if they require soaking. Generally, they do not nowadays and their cooking is a simple matter of simmering for about 20 minutes. Make sure they retain a little bite.

Serves 4

Ingredients

60g/2oz butter
1 tablespoon olive oil
$^1/_2$ Spanish onion, very finely chopped
2 cloves of garlic, finely chopped
$^1/_2$ large red pepper, deseeded and finely chopped
1 small green pepper, deseeded and finely chopped
2 teaspoons dried crushed chillies
freshly ground black pepper
2 medium tomatoes, peeled and finely chopped
salt
170g/6oz/$^3/_4$ cup green lentils, prepared, cooked and drained according to packet instructions
225g/$^1/_2$ lb *ev erişteşi* (Turkish pasta) or fusilli or farfalle or short-cut elbow macaroni, cooked and drained
2 teaspoons finely chopped fresh dill to garnish

1 In a heavy, high-sided sauté pan, or a medium saucepan, heat the butter and oil, sauté the onion and garlic gently for about 2 minutes or until softened slightly.
2 Add the red and green pepper, dried crushed chillies and black pepper. Stir to combine. When, after about 4 minutes, the mixture looks soft and translucent, add the tomatoes. Stir everything around briskly for about 1 minute. Add salt to taste.
3 Put the cooked, drained lentils into a large saucepan. Stir in the cooked, drained pasta and then the vegetable mixture. Over a low to medium heat, stir all the ingredients together until they are distributed evenly. Check seasoning. Cover with a lid briefly for 2 minutes, then serve garnished with fresh dill.

Pasta with Spinach and Yogurt

Best results come from spinach which is cut into longish shreds, so buy large-leafed spinach rather than the baby type. Although in the European kitchen the main ingredients of pasta and spinach would be bound in cream, in Turkey yogurt is used. Yogurt accentuates – rather than masks – the fresh taste of the spinach, while providing a healthier dish.

Serves 4

Ingredients

455g/1lb *ev eriştesi* (Turkish pasta) or elbow macaroni or tagliatelle or linguine
salt
30g/1oz butter
2 tablespoons olive oil
2 large cloves of garlic, very finely chopped
225g/$^1/_2$ lb spinach, finely shredded and washed
455g/1lb yogurt
1 tablespoon double cream (optional)
a good pinch of chilli powder
1$^1/_2$ tablespoons finely chopped fresh dill

1 Cook the pasta in a large saucepan of boiling salted water until done to your liking; drain.
2 In a separate, large saucepan, heat the butter and oil, then sauté the garlic for 1 minute over a medium heat.
3 Add the spinach, yogurt and cream, and quickly stir everything around. Add the drained pasta, and stir for 1–2 minutes over high heat to combine.
4 Pile on to serving plates and scatter with chilli powder and fresh dill.

Pasta with Walnuts

A minimalist approach to pasta can produce brilliant results. Occasionally, I like to bid farewell to the clutter of many ingredients and, instead, let pasta work as a calm, blank canvas, throwing a single element – in this case, walnuts – into powerfully sharp relief. This understated dish becomes all the more elegant when accompanied by a salad of peppery rocket and crisp chicory.

Serves 2

Ingredients

225g/^{1}/$_2$ lb *ev eriştesi* (Turkish pasta) or fusilli or farfalle
salt
9 tablespoons walnut oil
7g/^{1}/$_4$ oz unsalted butter
115g/4oz/1 cup walnut pieces
freshly ground black pepper
1^1/$_2$ teaspoons finely chopped fresh dill or flat-leaf parsley

1 Cook the pasta, until done to your liking, in plenty of boiling salted water to which you have added 1 tablespoon of the walnut oil. Drain.
2 Return the pasta to the pan and shake it briefly over high heat until any excess water has evaporated.

Remove the pan from the heat and stir in the butter, the remaining walnut oil and the walnuts. Grind over black pepper and add salt to taste.
3 Pile on to individual plates, scatter with the fresh herbs of your choice and serve straight away.

Pasta with Sucuk and Eggs

Eggs with sausage, and eggs with bacon, are classic partnerships. They explain the success of Italy's *pasta alla carbonara* – and also Turkey's Pasta with Sucuk and Eggs. Sucuk is a velvet-textured, spicy, lamb-based, dried sausage available from Turkish grocers. Other types of smooth-surfaced dried sausage may be substituted, as long as it lends itself to being diced. Cervelat, leberkäse, loukanika and fine-textured salamis work well.

Serves 4

Ingredients

455g/1lb *ev eriştesi* (Turkish pasta) or fusilli or penne or elbow macaroni
salt
40g/1$\frac{1}{2}$ oz butter
340g/12oz sucuk or other dried sausage, cut into large dice
2 large egg yolks
2 tablespoons double cream
freshly ground black pepper
2$\frac{1}{2}$ tablespoons finely chopped fresh dill

1 Cook the pasta in plenty of boiling salted water until done to your liking; drain.
2 While the pasta is cooking, heat the butter in a large sauté pan or saucepan. When the butter foams, add the sausage and stir to coat it. Cover and leave to cook gently for 5 minutes. Meanwhile, whisk together the egg yolks and cream. Season to taste and set aside briefly.
3 Stir the cooked drained pasta into the saucepan containing the sausage. Shake the pan briefly over heat to ensure that the pasta is hot. Off the heat, pour the yolks and cream over the pasta and stir well with a wooden spoon to distribute the egg mixture evenly. The heat of the pasta should set the egg mixture lightly to give a creamy sauce. Check seasoning.
4 Pile on to individual plates. Scatter with fresh dill and serve straight away.

Pasta with Aubergine and Red Vegetables

Soaking the aubergine in salted water makes it cook faster and thus, in turn, assures a juicy quality. At Sofra, the pasta we use for this lively-looking dish is *eriste*, a Turkish pasta with a natural, creamy colour and a short, slender cut. However, a red, tomato-flavoured pasta or even a green, spinach-flavoured one can be used as long as its shape is small. Bows, twists and corkscrews are all acceptable.

Serves 4

Ingredients

1 medium aubergine, peeled and diced
salt
$^{1}/_{2}$ Spanish onion, finely chopped
2 medium cloves of garlic, finely chopped
4 tablespoons olive oil
$^{1}/_{2}$ red pepper, deseeded and finely chopped
4 medium tomatoes, peeled and coarsely chopped
1 teaspoon dried crushed chillies
about 225ml/8fl oz/1 cup water
freshly ground black pepper
455g/1lb *ev eriştesi* (Turkish pasta) or fusilli, or farfalle or cavatappi
2 tablespoons finely chopped fresh flat-leaf parsley (optional)

1 Soak the aubergine pieces in heavily salted water for 15–20 minutes. Drain, rinse well, then drain again and dry on kitchen towels.
2 In a large saucepan, sauté the onion and garlic in the oil over a medium heat. After 2 minutes, stir in the red pepper and the aubergine. Stir to combine then, after 1 minute, mix in the tomatoes. Add the chilli, almost all of the water and seasoning to taste.
3 Cover with a lid and leave to simmer for about 12 minutes or until the liquid reduces to a sauce.

During this time, check progress occasionally and stir. If the sauce looks too thick, add the rest of the water.
4 Meanwhile, cook the pasta in a large saucepan of boiling salted water until done to your liking; drain.
5 Stir the drained pasta into the sauce, mixing carefully to combine the ingredients without breaking them up.
6 Pile the pasta on to individual plates and serve just as it is or with some fresh flat-leaf parsley.

Pasta with Seafood

Here, I have given tiger prawns and baby squid flavours which are indebted to the Far East. Oriental seasonings have always had a big influence on Turkish cookery. This is chiefly because of Istanbul's history as a key trading centre for spices travelling from the Far East to western Europe.

Serves 4

Ingredients

4 tablespoons olive oil
$1/2$ large Spanish onion, finely chopped
2 cloves of garlic, finely chopped
200g/7oz uncooked tiger prawns
salt
$1/2$ tablespoon cornflour
4 tablespoons sesame oil
1 tablespoon grated or chopped fresh ginger root
285g/10oz baby squid, cleaned and cut into rings
1 red pepper, deseeded and cut into matchsticks
115g/4oz shii-take or oyster mushrooms, sliced
1 small bunch spring onions, trimmed and cut diagonally into thirds
2 small, green, mild chilli peppers, deseeded and finely chopped
1 tablespoon Thai fish sauce diluted with 2 tablespoons water
2 tablespoons rice vinegar
170g/6oz ev eriştesi (Turkish pasta) or farfalle or fusilli or cavatappi, cooked and drained
1 tablespoon finely chopped fresh coriander

1 Heat the olive oil in a large saucepan. Gently sweat the onion and garlic for about 7 minutes or until soft and translucent.
2 Meanwhile, sprinkle the prawns with salt, coat with the cornflour and, in a small bowl, turn them in 2 tablespoons of the sesame oil. Heat the remaining sesame oil in a frying pan and sauté the prawns for 1–2 minutes, turning them as they change colour. Remove and set aside.
3 When the onion is soft, stir in the ginger, squid and red pepper, then the mushrooms, spring onions, chilli peppers, Thai fish sauce and the rice vinegar. Cover, and simmer over a low to medium heat for 1–2 minutes, shaking the pan occasionally.
4 Add the reserved prawns and the cooked drained pasta. Stir briefly to combine and warm through. Arrange on plates. Add fresh coriander and serve.

Feta Cheese

Turkish feta cheese is a beautiful thing – smooth, easy to grate into silky strands, and with an attractive piquancy to its flavour rather than an overwhelming saltiness. Like all feta cheese, its special flavour comes from a ripening process in brine or salt. Grated Turkish feta melds beautifully with short strands, or small shapes, of creamy, undersalted pasta; and, in the resultant exchange of flavours, a refreshing raciness emerges. If you shop around, you will find Turkish feta in Turkish food stores.

More widely available is packaged Greek feta which appears on most supermarket shelves. This is crumblier and saltier than its fresh Turkish counterpart. To get the best out of Greek feta, buy a good-quality pack well within the scope of its sell-by date. At home, it can be made less salty by soaking it in milky water.

Pasta with Feta

To offset the salty astringency of the feta, I omit salt from the cooking water of the pasta. Turkish dried pasta is fairly glutinous, so I include a little oil in the water to prevent sticking. Fresh dill gives this dish a vivacious finish.

Serves 4

Ingredients

455g/1lb *ev eriştesi* (Turkish pasta) or short-cut elbow macaroni or farfalle or fusilli
a small amount of vegetable oil
115g/4oz unsalted butter
1 teaspoon dried crushed chillies
1 teaspoon dried oregano
170g/6oz/1$^1/_2$ cups feta cheese, grated into longish strands
1$^1/_2$ tablespoons finely chopped fresh dill or fresh flat-leaf parsley

1 Cook the pasta, until done to your liking, in a large saucepan of boiling water to which you have added a few drops of oil; drain.

2 In a deep-sided sauté pan or a large saucepan, heat the butter over a fairly high heat until it foams.

3 Add the chilli, oregano and the drained pasta. Stir around for 2–3 minutes.

4 Pile on to serving plates. Add the grated feta and herbs, then serve straight away.

Pasta with a Lamb and Tomato Sauce

Pasta unites here with a rich, gently-simmered sauce of minced lamb, tomatoes and Mediterranean vegetables. A touch of oregano and chilli gives the dish a Turkish exuberance. For the pasta, choose tubes or shells to hold the sauce.

Serves 4

Ingredients

5 tablespoons olive oil
1 Spanish onion, finely chopped
2 cloves of garlic, finely chopped
340g/12oz minced lamb
$1/2$ small red pepper, deseeded and finely chopped
$1/2$ small green pepper, deseeded and finely chopped
2 mild green chilli peppers, deseeded and finely chopped
3 teaspoons tomato purée
1kg/2lb 4oz tomatoes, peeled and coarsely chopped
2 tablespoons dried oregano
about $1/2$ teaspoon dried crushed chillies (optional)
200ml/7fl oz/$3/4$ cup chicken stock
salt and freshly ground black pepper
285g/10oz *kalem* (Turkish pasta) or penne or conchigilie
2 teaspoons finely chopped fresh oregano or flat-leaf parsley

1 In a large saucepan, heat the oil and sweat the onion and garlic for about 7 minutes or until soft and translucent.

2 Stir in the lamb, turning it until it has coloured evenly. Stir in the red, green and chilli peppers, the tomato purée, tomatoes, dried oregano and the dried crushed chillies if desired. When the tomatoes have flopped, add the chicken stock. Season to taste. Cover the pan and simmer gently, using a heat diffusing mat, for 30–40 minutes.

3 Just before serving, cook the pasta in plenty of boiling salted water until done to your liking. Drain the pasta and toss it with the lamb sauce. Scatter with the fresh herbs and serve.

Pide Dough

Pide dough, known in Europe as pizza dough, is fantastically quick and easy to make; and the 15 minutes or so of time invested offers great rewards: the finished crust is crisper and tastier than any commercial counterpart; the toppings can be wild, resourceful or just plain personal; and any superfluous dough can be frozen and put on hold for an emergency. Use the sort of fast action yeast that you can just throw in with the flour.

Makes 4 x 170g/6oz portions of pide dough, each one enough for a pide for 1–2 persons

Ingredients

455g/1lb/3^1/$_4$ cups strong white plain flour
2 teaspoons salt
1 × 7g/^{1}/$_4$ oz sachet fast action dried yeast
about 285ml/^{1}/$_2$ pint/1^1/$_3$ cups warm water
a small amount of flour for kneading and rolling
a small amount of vegetable oil
1 egg yolk
a small amount of milk

1 Sift the flour and salt into a large mixing bowl. Sprinkle in the yeast. Gradually add all but a few tablespoons of the warm water, mixing by hand to form a ball of stiff dough. Add the last few tablespoons of water only if needed to make the dough cohere.
2 Turn the dough on to a lightly floured surface. Knead for 10 minutes or until the dough is unsticky and elastic.
3 Return the dough to a clean, dry bowl. Cover the dough closely with a warm damp cloth. Leave it in a warm place for 1 hour or until the dough has doubled its bulk.
4 Knead the dough for a few seconds and roll it into a sausage shape, about 30cm/12 inches long. Cut the dough crosswise into 4 equal portions, each weighing about 170g/6oz. Wrap any portions which are not for immediate use in clingfilm, then freeze them until required.

5 On a lightly floured surface, roll out a portion of dough to a shape which suits the equipment you have to hand: if you have a special, shallow baking tin, 25–30cm/10–12 inches in diameter, then oil it and line it with a circle of rolled-out dough about 18cm/7 inches in diameter. If you do not have a special tin, then roll a rough oval measuring about 23 × 13 cm/9 × 5 inches, and transfer it to a lightly oiled, flat baking sheet.
6 Set the rolled-out dough aside, uncovered, in a warm place, to prove for about 30 minutes.
7 With your fingertips, stretch the dough outwards to make a larger shape – you will be able to do this now without the dough springing back. Brush the surface with a little oil, then turn the pide over. If you like, brush the edge with a little beaten egg yolk and milk. Add the topping of your choice to the pide and bake it *(see pages 110–113)*.

Kıymalı Pide

The topping here of spiced minced lamb is hot but clean, due to a bracing boost of fresh dill and parsley. It is a popular Turkish mixture. Its secret lies in the fine-chopping of the ingredients. At Sofra, we chop by hand, but you can use a food processor if you prefer. The final raw mixture must cohere easily, and feel soft and moist. In Turkey, two eggs are sometimes added to the topping towards the end of cooking.

Serves 1–2

Ingredients

170g/6oz pide dough *(see page 109)*
455g/1lb finely ground minced lamb
1 medium Spanish onion, very finely chopped
2 small Charleston peppers or $\frac{1}{2}$ large red or green pepper, deseeded and finely chopped
3 medium tomatoes, peeled and finely chopped
2 teaspoons dried crushed chillies
salt and ground white pepper
freshly ground black pepper
2 tablespoons finely chopped fresh dill
3 tablespoons finely chopped fresh flat-leaf parsley
a few strips of pepper to garnish
a few slices of tomato to garnish
2 eggs (optional)
a small amount of melted butter

1 Have ready the pide dough, rolled out *(see steps 1–6, page 109)*.

2 In a large mixing bowl, combine the lamb, onion, pepper(s), tomatoes, dried crushed chillies, seasoning and fresh herbs. If the mixture does not cohere easily, gradually add up to 2 tablespoons of water.

3 Spread the mixture over the pide. Garnish the top with strips of pepper and slices of tomato.

4 Bake in an oven preheated to 230°C/450°F/gas mark 8 for 12 minutes or until done. Towards the end of the cooking, add 2 eggs to the top of the lamb mixture if desired.

5 When the pide is done to your liking, brush its edge with melted butter and serve.

Pastırma Pide

Pastırma, a type of Turkish cured beef – spiced and air-dried to concentrated beefiness – is delicious when combined with egg, as here. In the absence of pastırma, Italian brassaola would be a good substitute.

Serves 1–2

Ingredients

170g/6oz pide dough *(see page 109)*
12 thin slices Turkish pastırma or other salted, air-dried beef
a small amount of olive oil
a small amount of beaten egg
1 egg

1 Have ready the pide dough, rolled out *(see steps 1–6, page 109)*.
2 Arrange the slices of cured beef on top and brush them very lightly with olive oil. Brush the edge of the pide with beaten egg. Make a small space between the slices in the middle. Break the whole egg into a cup and slide it, yolk and white intact, into the middle of the pide.
3 Bake in an oven preheated to 230°C/450°F/gas mark 8 for 7–10 minutes or until the dough is crisp and the egg cooked.
4 Serve the pide just as it is.

Kaşarlı Pide

Melted cheese and lightly cooked egg are combined in a way which gives this pide the appearance of fluffy clouds. The egg should be beaten minimally so that white and yolk are unevenly blended and poised to produce variegated shades of colour and texture. Any flavoursome, hard or semi-hard cheese which melts down smoothly can be employed.

Serves 1–2

Ingredients

170g/6oz pide dough *(see page 109)*
1–2 tablespoons milk
85g/3oz/³/₄ cup grated kasar peyniri (Turkish cheese) or other grated hard cheese such as Gruyère or Cheddar
2 eggs, lightly beaten

1 Have ready the pide dough, rolled out *(see steps 1–6, page 109)*.
2 Brush the dough generously with the milk. Scatter over the cheese and dribble the beaten egg on top. Spread the egg mixture with a brush or with fingers to ensure that it covers the surface area of cheese.
3 Bake in an oven preheated to 230°C/450°F/gas mark 8 for 7–10 minutes or until the dough is crisp and the egg lightly cooked.
4 Serve the pide just as it is.

Kuşbaşılı Pide

Small morsels of tender succulent lamb lie at the heart of this luxury pide. For the pide to be true to its exalted reputation, only eye-of-loin fillet of lamb should be used. The meat should be chopped very finely – never minced; and the chopping is best done by hand rather than by machine. Unless machine blades are razor sharp, they squeeze meat fibres and reduce succulence.

Serves 1–2

Ingredients

170g/6oz pide dough *(see page 109)*
170g/6oz eye-of-loin fillet of lamb, very finely chopped
115g/4oz Spanish onion, finely chopped
about 7g/^{1}/$_4$ oz butter
3 small tomatoes, peeled and finely chopped
1 large Charleston pepper, deseeded and finely chopped
^{1}/$_2$ teaspoon dried crushed chillies
1 teaspoon finely chopped fresh flat-leaf parsley
salt
^{1}/$_2$ teaspoon freshly ground black pepper
1 egg lightly beaten

1 Have ready the pide dough, rolled out *(see steps 1–6, page 109)*.
2 In a large mixing bowl, combine the lamb with all the remaining ingredients except for the egg.
3 Spread the lamb mixture over the pide. Brush the edge of the pide with the beaten egg. Brush any remaining egg very lightly over the surface of the lamb mixture.
4 Bake in an oven preheated to 230°C/450°F/gas mark 8 for 10–12 minutes or until cooked.
5 Serve the pide just as it is.

Desserts and
Turkish Specialities

Sütlaç

I am loathe to describe Sütlaç as a rice pudding – though that is what it is – partly because of the unfortunate connotations in English and partly because the dessert depends on such a small proportion of rice. It contains no eggs and only a touch of cream; so it is altogether a surprisingly light affair, eaten slightly chilled from dainty dishes. In Turkey, we include some mastica, a peculiar resinous substance which exudes the wonderful scent of natural pine. In its absence, you might like to use a little extra rosewater and lemon zest to boost the element of fragrance.

Serves 10–12

Ingredients

115g/4oz/^{1}/$_2$ cup plus 2 tablespoons Basmati rice
1.7 litres/3 pints/7^1/$_2$ cups milk
300g/10^1/$_2$ oz/1^1/$_2$ cups caster sugar
2 teaspoons rosewater
3 tablespoons double cream
4 small pieces mastica (optional)
5 tablespoons cornflour
grated zest of ^{1}/$_2$ lemon

1 Cook the rice in simmering water for about 12 minutes or until just tender; drain and set aside.
2 In a large saucepan, heat to boiling point 1.4 litres/2^1/$_2$ pints/6^1/$_3$ cups of the milk, stirring in the sugar, rosewater, double cream, and mastica if used. While the milk heats, mix together in a basin the remaining cold milk and the cornflour, whisking until smooth.
3 When the hot milk mixture rises to the boil, adjust the heat to maintain a simmer. Stir in the drained rice and, in a steady stream, the cornflour mixture. Stir with a balloon whisk, moving it across the bottom of the pan, pressing lightly to mash the rice.

After about 10 minutes, the mixture should thicken to the consistency of thin cream and start to pull on the whisk. Stir in the lemon zest.
4 Ladle the rice into individual, ovenproof dishes placed in a roasting tin or in a shallow ovenproof dish. Add enough cold water to the container to immerse the dishes by two-thirds of their depth.
5 Place the container beneath a hot grill, or on the top shelf of an oven preheated to 475°F/240°C/gas mark 9, for 5 minutes or until the tops of the puddings turn golden brown.
6 Remove the puddings, set them aside to cool, then transfer them to a refrigerator. Serve chilled.

Kazandibi

This very white, fragile, milk and cream pudding which trembles beneath its dark caramelized crust, is a very ancient example of burnt cream – versions of which include the crème brulée of today's European cuisine.

Serves 6–8

Ingredients

1.14 litres/2 pints/5 cups milk
100g/3¹/₂ oz/¹/₂ cup caster sugar
2 small pieces mastica, finely chopped (optional)
1 teaspoon rosewater
2 tablespoons double cream
6 tablespoons cornflour
several good pinches of ground cinnamon

1 In a large saucepan, heat to boiling point 850ml/1¹/₂ pints/3³/₄ cups of the milk, stirring in the sugar, mastica, rosewater and double cream. While the milk heats, mix together in a basin the remaining cold milk and the cornflour, whisking until smooth.

2 When the hot milk rises to the boil, adjust the heat to a simmer, and gradually whisk in the cornflour mixture. Simmer for 12–15 minutes, stirring frequently with a whisk, until the mixture has the consistency of thin cream and does not dribble readily from the whisk. Keep the mixture warm over a very low heat using a heat-diffusing mat.

3 Set a warm shallow tin, about 22cm/8¹/₂ inches × 30cm/12 inches over a high heat on top of the stove. Add several tablespoons of the kazandibi to the hot tin and, with a firm, sharp spatula (or 7.5cm/3 inch decorator's scraper), push around the kazandibi until it has spread and burned itself out on the bottom of the tin. The aim is to obtain a burnt crust. When one part of the tin displays an appropriate burnt crust, turn the tin and burn another section until the whole tin is coated in a crust.

4 Off the heat, ladle the kazandibi into the tin and level the surface. Leave to cool, then transfer to a refrigerator. After about 30 minutes, the pudding will be firm to the touch and ready to serve. With a sharp knife mark the surface into either squares or rectangles for portions. Use a very sharp spatula (or decorator's scraper) to remove each portion complete with a burnt crust. Invert the portions on to plates, burnt-side uppermost. Sprinkle with cinnamon and serve on its own or with cherries, strawberries or grapes.

Apricots with Yogurt and Honey

This dish is a decorative combination of yogurt and fruit. Although dried apricots are featured here, the fruit can vary. Bananas, strawberries and grapes are among Turkey's favourite choices. The success of this particular version is due to an especially compatible alliance of flavours: dried apricots, almonds, pistachios, honey and, of course, top-quality cow's milk yogurt.

Serves 4

Ingredients

20 (about 170g/6oz/1 cup) dried apricots, soaked according to packet instructions
32 (about 40g/1^1/$_2$ oz/^{1}/$_4$ cup) whole, blanched almonds
400g/14oz natural yogurt (not the set variety)
4 tablespoons clear honey
2 tablespoons finely chopped pistachio kernels

1 Simmer the apricots with just enough water to cover until plump and tender. Drain through a sieve set over a bowl and reserve the cooking liquid. Rinse the apricots under cold water to cool them. Drain thoroughly.
2 Put one whole almond inside each apricot. Mix together the yogurt, honey and about 2 tablespoons of the reserved apricot cooking liquid.
3 Spread enough of the yogurt mixture on to a large circular serving plate to make an even bed. Place about 9 apricots around the border, making an outer circle. Put another apricot in the middle. Put a layer of yogurt on top, spreading it slightly with a spatula. Use the remaining apricots to make an inner circle. Decorate with the remaining 12 almonds. Cover the visible surface of yogurt with the chopped pistachios.
4 Serve the yogurt at room temperature or slightly chilled, allowing about 5 apricots per person.

Apricots

Apricots, fresh and dried, are used widely in Turkish dessert cookery and are a familiar addition to savoury dishes too. Their acceptance as a desirable, wholesome food, dates back to when the Romans obtained the fresh apricot, the *prunus armeniaca*, from the Far East via Armenia.

Fresh apricots are a rich source of vitamins C and A, and carotene; and although any drying process tends to diminish the vitamin C, the other valuable nutrients remain. Dried apricots from health-food shops are most likely to be sun dried. Those from supermarkets may have had their drying assisted by sulphur dioxide. The packet will inform you. Also available are the 'sugar-cured', or 'ready-to-eat', varieties. Although these officially require no soaking, they nevertheless profit from a little simmering to plump them up to a desirable size for recipes such this one and Kayısı Tatlısı *(page 123)*.

Depending on their producer, dried apricots which are not 'ready-to-eat' vary enormously in their required soaking and simmering time. Soaking ranges from 40 minutes to overnight, for example; so it is always worth reading the packet instructions. At Sofra, we soak the apricots overnight, starting them off in hot water. This reduces their cooking time the next day to a mere 10 minutes.

Yogurt Ring Mould with Cardamom, Rosewater and Lime

Impressively low in calories, this shimmering creation of yogurt and flavourings bears nothing of the 'plain Jane' image usually associated with healthy desserts. Lightly set and turned out of a ring mould, the yogurt acquires a trembling elegance. Its flavourings of cardamom, rosewater and lime combine to tease the palate with nuances of exotic fragrance. Serve it on its own or with grapes, a fruit salad (see pages 124–5) or strawberies and peaches bound with a peach purée.

Serves 6–8 (fills a 1.3 litre/2¼ pint ring mould)

Ingredients

1 heaped tablespoon cardamom pods
140ml/5fl oz/ ²/₃ cup milk
1 tablespoon caster sugar
2 × 500g/1lb 2oz cartons natural yogurt (not the set variety)
5 tablespoons rosewater
finely grated zest of ¹/₂ lime
2 medium egg whites
salt
5 teaspoons powdered gelatine

1 Slit open the cardamom pods, pick out the seeds and lightly crush them using a pestle and mortar or a rolling pin. Put the seeds and the milk in a saucepan set over a low heat. When the milk comes up to the boil, remove it from the heat, cover and leave to infuse for several hours.

2 Strain the milk through a fine nylon sieve into a bowl. Retain the seeds and pound these briefly with the sugar. In a large bowl, whisk together the yogurt, the milk, the seed and sugar mixture, the rosewater and the grated zest of lime. In a separate bowl, whisk together the egg whites with a pinch of salt until they form soft peaks; set aside briefly.

3 Thoroughly dissolve the gelatine in half a cup of very hot water. Let it cool slightly then stir it into the yogurt mixture. Quickly fold about one-third of the yogurt mixture into the beaten egg white, then tip the egg white mixture into the remaining yogurt mixture. Stir to combine evenly.

4 Tip the mixture into a 1.3 litre/2¼ pint ring mould. Level out the contents. Cover with an overturned plate and chill for 4 hours or until set.

5 When you are ready to serve, run a knife around the edge of the ring, then invert it onto a flat serving plate. Press the surface area of the ring with a cloth wetted in hot water. Lift away the ring. If the ring does not slip off, repeat the procedure. Serve the yogurt ring on its own or with its centre filled with a fruit salad.

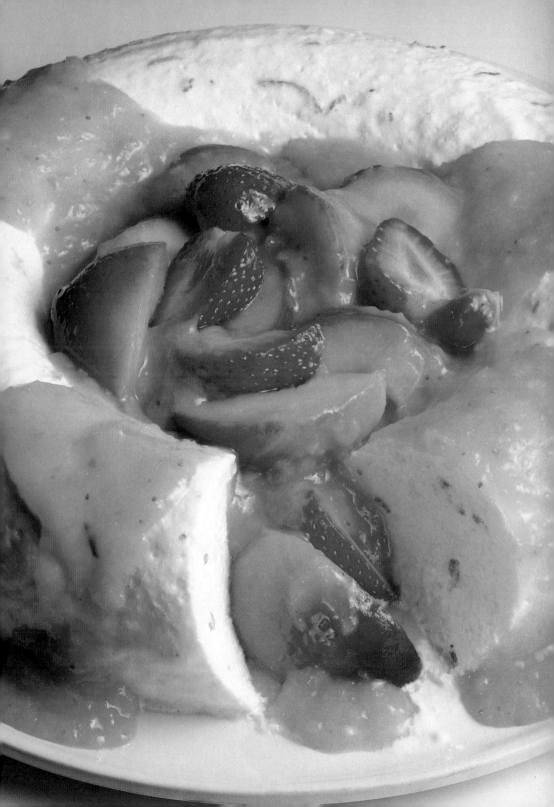

Kadayıf

Made with fine shreds of pastry resembling vermicelli, Turkish kadayıf is a dessert of great repute, and known in Arab countries as *künefe*. The pastry encloses a fresh, cream cheese filling; and the whole thing is drenched in fragrant syrup and embellished with walnuts. Because the dough can now be bought from supermarkets, as well as from Turkish grocers, the dessert is accessible to the home cook.

Serves 6

Ingredients

225g/¹/₂ lb/1 cup plus 2 tablespoons caster sugar
285ml/¹/₂ pint/1¹/₃ cups water
1 teaspoon rosewater
255g/9oz kadayıf dough
225g/¹/₂ lb butter
310g/11oz Turkish Nor cheese or ricotta, mashed
4–5 tablespoons walnuts, finely chopped

1 Put the sugar and water into a heavy-based saucepan. Stir over gentle heat, and when the sugar has dissolved, stop stirring, raise the heat and bring the syrup to the boil. Let the syrup boil for 5 minutes, then stand the base of the pan in cold water to arrest cooking. When the syrup is cool, stir in the rosewater.

2 Spread out the kadayıf dough on a large flat dish or baking tin. Melt the butter and drizzle all but 3 tablespoons of it over the dough. With your fingers, work lightly to separate the strands of dough and moisten them with the butter. Continue until all the dough has turned from white to pale gold.

3 Arrange half the dough in an even layer in a non-stick frying pan about 25cm/10 inches in diameter. Add the cheese in an even layer. Spread the remaining dough over the cheese and drizzle the remaining butter on top. Lightly flatten the whole thing, ideally with a smaller frying pan; otherwise use your hand. Cover with a lid.

4 Set the layered kadayıf over low heat and cook it for 20–25 minutes, or until crisp and golden. During this time, turn it every 5 minutes, inverting it on to a plate and slipping it back into the frying pan.

5 Transfer to a large serving plate. Scatter with walnuts and ladle over the syrup, making a small pool around the edge of the pastry. Cut into portions using a very sharp knife. Kadayıf is particularly good served hot, especially if you offer hazelnut or vanilla ice cream as an accompaniment. It is also excellent cold, and it keeps well.

Easy Almond Cake

You can put this cake together in next to no time, especially if you do the blending (step 2) in a food processor. The cake keeps well, so is worth making in a large quantity. It is also very versatile: good on its own, with yogurt, with fruit or – most delicious – with a purée of dried apricots.

Serves 10–12

Ingredients

1–2 tablespoons melted butter
170g/6oz unsalted butter, softened
200g/7oz/1 cup caster sugar
4 large eggs
140g/5oz/1²/₃ cups ground almonds
70g/2¹/₂ oz/¹/₂ cup plain flour, sifted
¹/₄ teaspoon almond flavouring
1–2 tablespoons sifted icing sugar, to decorate

1 Prepare a 23cm/9 inch cake tin: brush with melted butter, then line the bottom with non-stick baking parchment paper. Brush the paper with melted butter and lightly coat with flour.
2 In a large bowl, or in a food processor, beat the butter until smooth, then gradually beat in the sugar until light and fluffy. Beat in the eggs one at a time, then gradually beat in the almonds. When the mixture is well amalgamated, fold in the flour and stir in the almond flavouring. Transfer the mixture to the prepared tin and tap the tin on the work surface to ensure even distribution.

3 Bake in an oven preheated to 180°C/350°F/gas mark 4 for about 35 minutes or until the cake is firm to the touch in the middle. Remove from the tin and cool on a wire rack.
4 Dredge the top of the cake with the sifted icing sugar. Or sift the sugar over 2cm/³/₄ inch wide strips of cardboard, arranged in stripes or diamonds on the top of the cake; this will give an attractive appearance when the strips are removed.

Kayısı Tatlısı

A familiar feature of the Turkish dessert trolley is the display of these plump, orangey-toned apricots with what appears to be a green and white stripe running down one side. These kayısı tatlısı owe their stripe to whipped cream and chopped pistachios. Sometimes, walnuts or almonds might replace the pistachios.

Serves 4

Ingredients

20 (about 170g/6oz/1 cup) dried apricots, soaked according to packet instructions
425ml/15fl oz/2 cups double cream
7 tablespoons icing sugar
about 7 tablespoons finely chopped pistachio kernels
20 whole almonds, blanched or toasted according to taste

1 Simmer the apricots in a saucepan with just enough water to cover until they are plump and tender. This will take from 10–30 minutes, depending on the type of dried apricots. Drain, rinse under cold water, then drain again.

2 Whip the cream and icing sugar together to form firm, slightly grainy peaks. Spread out the pistachios on a plate. One by one, take an apricot, locate its hollow and pull the side seam gently apart to open up the apricot like a book. Place an almond in the middle, then use a knife to fill the centre of the almond with cream. Almost close the apricot. The cream should ooze out along the seam. If it does not, add a little more. Dip the exposed line of cream into the pistachios. Repeat with the remaining apricots.

3 Transfer the apricots to a flat dish and serve within 3 hours. In the meantime, keep them in a cool place. Serve on their own or with Turkish coffee.

Compote of Apricots, Prunes and Oranges

Although this salad combines dried and fresh fruit, its flavours work harmoniously. It is an extremely versatile assembly, as suited to the breakfast table as to the lunch or dinner setting. Make sure that you remove all pith from the oranges, cutting horizontally round each orange to remove skin and pith together in a continuous spiral.

Serves 4–6

Ingredients

225g/¹/₂ lb dried, ready-to-eat apricots
225g/¹/₂ lb dried, ready-to-eat pitted prunes
455g/1lb/2¹/₄ cups caster sugar
570ml/1 pint/2¹/₂ cups water
2 large oranges, free of peel and pith, and sliced
2 tablespoons clear honey
30g/1oz/¹/₄ cup walnut pieces

1 Put the dried fruit and sugar into a large saucepan. Pour over the water. Bring to a simmer, stirring gently to dissolve the sugar. Partially cover the pan and let the mixture simmer gently for 12 minutes, adding a little more water to the pan if the fruit ceases to be immersed in liquid.

2 Add the slices of orange and stir in the honey. Simmer for a further 5 minutes.

3 Arrest the cooking by standing the base of the pan in cold water. When the compote is cold, transfer it to a serving bowl. Cover and chill for at least 1 hour. Add the walnuts just before serving. Offer yogurt as an accompaniment.

Peach, Nectarine and Fresh Fig Compote

In this salad of natural goodness, the syrup is flavoured with the skins of the peaches and nectarines. I choose only fruit with very pink skins so that when they are boiled in the syrup, they give it a natural pink blush. Quartered fresh figs are a ravishing addition but the salad can hold its own without them. For full appreciation of flavours, serve at room temperature or chilled just slightly.

Serves 6–8

Ingredients

340g/12oz/1$^3/_4$ cups caster sugar
425ml/15fl oz/2 cups water
3 large, firm peaches, skins removed and reserved, the fruit cut into eighths
4 large, firm nectarines, skins removed and reserved, the fruit cut into eighths
1 tablespoon lemon juice
4 fresh figs, quartered
2–3 tablespoons slivered almonds
a few rose petals to decorate (optional)

1 Put the sugar and water into a heavy-based saucepan large enough to hold the fruit. Over low heat, stir to dissolve the sugar. When you can see clearly the bottom of the pan, stop stirring, raise the heat and bring the syrup to the boil.
2 Adjust the heat to maintain a simmer. Add the peaches and nectarines and simmer them gently until the fruit is tender without losing its shape. This will take from 3–15 minutes depending on the ripeness of the fruit. Remove pieces of fruit as they are done with a slotted spoon; transfer to a plate to cool.
3 When you have removed all the peaches and nectarines from the syrup, raise the heat, add the reserved fruit skins to the syrup and boil it hard for at least 5 minutes or until the skins have given up their flavour and colour to the syrup. Strain the syrup through a sieve set over a bowl, then leave it to cool completely.
4 Add the lemon juice, fresh figs, peaches and nectarines and turn the fruit in the syrup gently. Scatter over the almonds and, if you wish, a few rose petals. Serve at room temperature or chilled slightly. Offer yogurt and almond biscuits as accompaniments.

Note

The best way to remove the skins of peaches and nectarines is to score their skin lightly around the middle, then plunge the fruit briefly into very hot water, then into cold. The skins will curl away easily.

Turkish Coffee

For kahve, or Turkish coffee, the beans must be pulverized to a powder. The type of bean you use, its roast and so on, are matters of personal preference, although some guidelines are given on the opposite page. Ground cinnamon or saffron, or a few cardamom seeds, can be scattered on top of the coffee just before serving. Although the recipe below mentions the use of a *cezve* or an *ibrik*, you can substitute a small saucepan. Sugar, assuming it is needed, is included and boiled with the coffee and water. Terms describe the desired sweetness. The ratio of sugar per cup is as follows:

sekerli/sweet:	1 heaped teaspoon or more
orta/medium sweet:	1 level teaspoon
sade/without sugar	

Serves 1

Ingredients

2 level, or 1 very heaped, teaspoons very finely ground coffee
1 small coffee cup water
caster sugar to taste *(see above)*

1 In a *cezve*, or *ibrik*, mix together the coffee and water, and the sugar as desired.
2 Set over low heat and bring to the boil. When the froth begins to rise, remove from the heat, stir, and let the froth subside.
3 Repeat step 2 twice more.
4 Pour into cups allowing a little froth for each cup. Do not stir or you will disturb the sediment. Allow the coffee to settle before drinking it.

Turkish Coffee

Kahve, or Turkish coffee, epitomizes for me the elegance of Turkish cuisine. There is something refined about the way in which the coffee is brewed to draw out only the purest, distilled juices of the coffee. It is the frothy juices – the so-called 'face of the coffee' – which are then consumed, leaving behind the sediment. The small cups in which the coffee is served remind us that less can be more. And the traditional implement in which the coffee is made, the long-handled *cezve* or *ibrik*, adds a note of ceremony which is often completed by a special serving tray engraved with religious messages and blessings.

Arabica beans are the main choice of bean for Turkish coffee. Among them, genuine mocha varieties from the Yemen are highly-prized. Kenya beans tend towards richness and acidity while Brazilian ones lean towards sweetness; a blend of these two produces a balance which suits some people very well. Generally a medium roast is chosen, since a high roast in such concentrated form as Turkish coffee is too sharp for many tastes.

Coffee-drinking is embedded into Turkish cultural life. Turks will sometimes take extra sugar with their coffee for a happy occasion such as a wedding, but no sugar to mark a bitter occasion such as a funeral. People will sit for hours over coffee exchanging ideas,

Turkish Tea

Always on hand, usually in a special two-chamber teapot, çay, or Turkish tea is poured into elegant tea glasses and consumed without milk. The two-chamber teapot, available in specialist shops, is a neat way of keeping spare hot water close to the brewed tea so that preferred tea strengths can be adjusted. Specialist shops will also stock Turkish tea. In its absence, however, virtually any tea which suits your personal taste is acceptable. For a strong, malty brew, for example, choose Assam. For a light, scented tea, choose jasmine.

Serves 4–6

Ingredients

about 1–1.2 litres/1¾–2 pints water
4–6 teaspoons tea leaves
sugar to taste

1 Fill the larger pot of a two-chamber teapot with water and bring to the boil.
2 Warm the smaller pot. Add the tea and pour over half the boiling water from the larger pot. Stir. Leave to stand for about 5 minutes. During this time, keep the remaining water hot, and warm the tea glasses.
3 To serve, put the smaller pot on top of the larger one. Fill each tea glass half-full with tea, then top it up with some of the remaining hot water from the larger pot. Offer sugar separately.

Clove Tea

In Turkey, tea can be flavoured with a variety of spices, among them cinnamon and aniseed. In the recipe here, the simple addition of cloves produces instantly delicious results. Sugar is optional although the addition of just half a teaspoon per cup brings out the distinctive taste of the tea. It is definitely not a tea for milk, though!

Serves 6

Ingredients

3 cloves, lightly crushed, preferably in a pestle and mortar
1¹/₂ tablespoons Darjeeling tea
1.2 litres/2 pints boiling water
sugar to taste (optional)

1 Put the cloves and the tea into a warmed teapot. Add the boiling water and stir.
2 Cover and leave to stand for 5 minutes.

3 Serve, pouring through a strainer. Offer sugar to taste.

Mint Tea

Mint tea is recognized universally as being a wonderful pick-me-up in hot weather. The taste can vary in subtle ways, however, depending on the type of tea and the mint employed. I find the teas which harmonize best with mint are Turkish teas, and Chinese jasmine, oolong and green gunpowder. Among the options for mint, you are bound to try first any mint which invades your garden. That said, spearmint (*Mentha spicata*), with pointed leaves, is a classic choice, while some people swear by apple mint (*Mentha rotundifolia*), and others by peppermint (*Mentha piperita*).

To make mint tea, follow the recipe for Turkish Tea *(see page 128)*, reducing the amount of tea leaves by 1 teaspoon and adding about 2 dozen mint leaves to the pot before pouring on the boiling water. When you pour the tea, add a sprig of mint to each glass.

Ayran

A chilled concoction of yogurt, water and mint, Ayran is a marvellously refreshing, healthy drink. In Istanbul, special street-vendors, or Ayrancı, are in evidence selling the drink until the early hours of the morning. Try it on a hot day and you will probably never touch a commercial fizzy drink again. You can make it in seven seconds in a blender.

Serves 2

Ingredients

1 × 200g/7oz carton natural yogurt
285ml/¹/₂ pint/1¹/₃ cups still or aerated water
1¹/₂ tablespoons dried mint
salt
crushed ice to serve (optional)
2 small sprigs fresh mint to garnish (optional)

1 Whisk together the yogurt, water and dried mint until well-blended and slightly foamy. If you like, do this in a blender or a food processor. Season to taste with salt. Transfer to a refrigerator until chilled.

2 Serve Ayran in tall tumblers, preferably poured over crushed ice. If you wish, add a garnish of fresh mint.

Boza

In Turkey, boza is more than the favourite drink for cold winter nights, it is part of the life of large cities, where it is sold by street-vendors until past midnight. To describe boza as being made of fermented bulgur, or stale bread, may sound off-putting; but I assure you it is wonderful, resembling milk in appearance yet offering a moreish, slightly nutty taste. Packed with nutrients, especially B vitamins, it is a good drink to have to hand if you anticipate missing lunch or eating dinner late. A pleasant, nutritious drink can also be made by following steps 1–3 of the recipe below, then sweetening the mixture to taste, and omitting the fermentation process. The result, however, could not be called boza.

Makes about 1.4 litres/2 ¹/₂ pints/6 ¹/₃ cups

Ingredients

225g/¹/₂ lb bulgur
2.5 litres/4¹/₂ pints/16 ¹/₃ cups water
1 teaspoon caster sugar
140ml/5fl oz/²/₃ cup hot water
1 tablespoon yeast
395g/14oz/2 cups caster sugar
milk (optional)
a few good pinches of ground cinnamon
a few roasted chick-peas (optional)

1. Put the bulgur and 1.7 litres/3 pints/7¹/₂ cups of the water into a large saucepan. Partially cover the pan and bring to the boil. Adjust the heat and simmer for about 50 minutes or until the bulgur is a liquid mush. During this time, add a further 850ml/1¹/₂ pints/3³/₄ cups of water in 2 or 3 stages, as and when the bulgur has absorbed most of the previous water.

2. Remove from the heat. Wrap a cloth around the saucepan and its lid. Leave it overnight in a warm place.

3. Purée the mixture in a blender.

4. Using a fine sieve over a large bowl, rub the mixture through the sieve using the edge of a wooden spoon, and scraping the underneath of the sieve frequently. What emerges should resemble a thick ivory-coloured milk. Discard the squeezed-out husk which collects in the sieve.

5. Dissolve the teaspoon of sugar in hot water. Sprinkle over the yeast and whisk briefly. Cover with clingfilm and put in a warm place for 15 minutes. Whisk again.

6. Stir the yeast, and then the remaining sugar, into the bulgur. Pour into glass jars or airtight containers, leaving a 1cm/¹/₂ inch space at the top. Close with lids.

7. Leave the containers in a warm, draught-free place, such as an airing cupboard, for 3 days. During this time, remove the lids and stir the boza at least once.

8. To serve, heat the boza gently. If you like, you can mix each serving with about one-third warm milk. Sprinkle with ground cinnamon and, if you wish to be authentic, serve with a few roasted chick-peas.

Olives with Flavourings and Bread

At home, I always keep some flavoured olives to hand. They can be eaten with crusty bread at almost any time of day; and they are ready to be offered to unexpected guests, along with a drink. Flavoured olives and bread also constitute my most typical breakfast menu. Try them as a relief from a breakfast of toast and jam; they will give your day a dynamic start. As a garnish, fresh dill offers an exhilarating lift which befits the breakfast table; but it is by no means essential.

Serves 2

Ingredients

115g/4oz/^{1}/$_2$ cup olives of your choice, drained of brine
3 tablespoons olive oil
^{1}/$_4$ teaspoon ground coriander
^{1}/$_2$ teaspoon dried oregano
a pinch of cayenne pepper
^{1}/$_2$ teaspoon finely chopped fresh dill (optional)
crusty bread to accompany

1 In a small flat dish, combine the olives with the oil, coriander, oregano and cayenne pepper. Mix to dissolve the dried herbs into the oil. Scatter over the dill if available. Ideally, set aside briefly so that flavours can intermingle.

2 To eat, tilt the dish slightly and use the bread to mop up the flavoured oil which collects at the edge. Eat the olives with the dipped bread.

Special Stirred Eggs with Sucuk Sausage

This is a variation on the theme of Special Stirred Eggs with Feta *(see page 15)*. The method is the same but I replace the diced feta with 55g/2oz of sliced sucuk, a type of Turkish garlic sausage which has a racy spiciness without being hot and aggressive. You can buy it from any Turkish store. Failing that, substitute an Italian, Danish or Hungarian salami or a Spanish chorizo. When I use sucuk, I omit both salt and pepper from the dish.

Fried or Grilled Sucuk
Although sucuk is a good partner for eggs *(above)*, it can also be enjoyed on its own and at any time of day. Simply brush as many slices as you require with melted butter or olive oil, then fry or grill them for about 1 minute. Eat with lots of good crusty bread.

All royalties from the Softa Cookbook will be donated to the author's Foundation in Turkey, Huseyin Ozer Egitim Ve Kultur Vakfi, set up to help support under privileged children in his hometown in Resadiye. If you would like to know more about the Foundation please contact:

Etim Dindjer
Sofra
40–42 King Street
Covent Garden
London WC2E 8JS

Tel: 0171 836 6655
Fax: 0171 836 4355

Index